YOU ARE A LIMITED EDITION

An inspiring collection of student lived experiences

YOU ARE A LIMITED EDITION

An inspiring collection of student lived
experiences
©TG Consulting Ltd
©Front cover illustration by Becky Willson

ISBN 9781912821822
A CIP catalogue record for this
book is available from the British Library.

Published 2021
Tricorn Books, Aspex
42 The Vulcan Building
Gunwharf Quays
Portsmouth PO1 3BF

YOU ARE A LIMITED EDITION

Contents

DEDICATION

This book is dedicated to every single individual who questions their worth and doubts their own abilities. Embrace your differences and channel your efforts into making the most of opportunities to become your best self. You are not alone. You are perfect.
YOU ARE A LIMITED EDITION.

FOREWORD

Tonia Galati, Director, TG Consulting Ltd

TG Consulting is an independent education consultancy, specialising in employability, student engagement and social mobility. We connect educators, students, and employers. Our ethos is to connect, collaborate and create.

At TG Consulting Ltd, we believe that everyone is worth the effort, time and energy needed to develop themselves. So, it was important for us to provide a platform for some of the young people we have worked with, to be able to share their struggles and experiences, so that they could see how far they have come and to celebrate their achievements. We also wanted to provide reassurance and support to others who may be going through similar experiences.

To everyone who has purchased this book, thank you for supporting our endeavours and helping us to create opportunity for all, regardless of the challenges and barriers they face. All proceeds from the sale of this book will go towards supporting students who face disadvantage, to help them to reach their career goals.

I am in awe of all our authors, as it takes real guts and courage to be vulnerable and share your insecurities. These stories of lived experiences and overcoming life challenges, show just how incredible these individuals are.

I am proud of every single one of our authors, for sharing their stories, for being vulnerable and for empowering and changing the lives of others. They are all heroes and a huge inspiration.

They really are a LIMITED EDITION.

Tonia Galati
Director
TG Consulting Ltd
www.tgconsultingltd.co.uk

These stories have been written in the students' own words and writing style. Editorial changes have been kept to a minimum, to retain the rawness of these real lived experiences.

Jeffrey A

Sharing my story has given me, for the first time, a chance to properly reflect on my own experience and the experience of others who come from similar backgrounds. I hope all who read it – whether senior executives or students – come to understand the importance of working together to increase access to all, regardless of their background or social-economic status.

Representation

At university, I would come to understand, through interactions with others, and reflections on my own personal experiences, the hidden challenges and the glaring roadblocks in the path of Black students like myself. By coming to understand my own story, and realising the similarities in the experiences of others, I would develop an acute sense of the world with two different lenses: how it saw me and how I saw it.

At school, my experience was fine. I now realise the full benefits of attending a school with people from different backgrounds, countries, ethnicities and religions. Some of my teachers were Black, and the benefits of engaging with them was clear: my first interaction of a mentoring session of sorts would come from my Black English teacher, who would go the extra mile to awaken my confidence and broaden the scope of my ambition. She was one of two Black teachers I would have at secondary school.

At the ages of 11–16, I would be relatively unbothered – perhaps through ignorance – of the lack of diversity in the school curriculum. Maybe, my interactions with friends from all corners of the world did well to offset that, and my strong cultural background at home would grant me the steady foundation I needed. So, whilst I may have been all too familiar about Henry VIII and his six wives, I also understood my own history and that of my family, well. My dad would often tell tales of the plight of slaves from Elmina, Ghana, the place of my Ghanaian heritage – and my mum would insist, sometimes against my will, on donning traditional African wear to a wedding or a friend's birthday party. As I've grown older, I have come to understand the intentional interventions to make me aware of my own culture and the history our curriculum too often avoids. Not every other Black boy or girl has the same opportunity, proving the overwhelming need to diversify our curriculum.

At sixth form, I would come to realise the negative impact of the lack of diversity. I attended school in a relatively wealthy area – and classmates, through their words and deeds would often expose their lack of awareness and plain ignorance. Although never directed at me, banterous remarks would often mask their ill-informed views, and school politics would often reveal inherent biases. During the initial stages of applying to universities, the different aspirations was clear: whilst most students were reaching for the stars, the few Black students in the sixth form, were mostly tempering their ambitions. That feeling which I knew well, has come to be termed 'imposter syndrome'. At times, it's an overwhelming feeling, despite evidence to the contrary (good grades, skills, etc.) that somehow, you're not right for that particular institution, role, or opportunity. Yes, it is something that is not unique to Black boys and girls – but its impact on them, and the opportunities so often denied as a result, must be acknowledged.

Some of this includes educational institutions and organisations working to actively increase diversity and representation. For example, as mentioned above, it was a Black teacher, who gave me my first mentoring session and instilled a degree of confidence and aspiration in me: after all, she had gone to a good university, achieved good grades and was practising her dream profession, so why couldn't I? It was her influence, and her work with myself and other students who she must have recognised herself in, that led to a persistence to work towards our dreams, whatever they may be. That is the true impact of representation. It might not show up in data or the statistics, but its impact is profound, and arguably, the most important.

Her influence, my experiences at sixth form and my strong foundation at home would propel me to university. During my first year, I would stumble throughout the year, with average grades and a cautious approach to the challenges and opportunities university offered. But like secondary school, that experience would be made so much easier by the people I had met – people who came from similar backgrounds and had similar stories. Just as had been the case in secondary school, it would also give me the chance to fix up and work towards achieving the best possible grades. Academically, it was my Black lecturers, just as my Black teacher in secondary school, who would insist that I could do better and force me to aspire for more.

After receiving my first first-grade essay, I would walk into my lecturer's office, with a degree of 'are you sure' surprise. She would offer a rebuke and warn me never to do that again. She would later explain, that in her experience of teaching, Black students would mostly second-guess their results, as if the mark they received was by mistake or luck. With that, I would gain new confidence, strike meaningful relationships with all lecturers and demand more of myself and them. During my final year, they would joke that they could tell it was me approaching their offices, because few others would come to ask about the improvements they could make, long after the day was finished. That new-found confidence and a willingness to achieve my true potential did not come out of thin air; instead, it came, once again, from someone who recognised the potential roadblocks in my path, and insisted, even demanded, that I do better.

Later on, I would go on to achieve my first-class, receiving the second-highest grade in my year. Nowhere in my transcripts will that conversation show up, nor will it read on my CV. But its impact can hardly be denied. It was a point at which I stopped questioning my own abilities and started working towards achieving more. That, and that alone, is the true power of representation; it's the ability to realise your potential in someone who might have grown up in a neighbourhood just like yours and experienced challenges so similar to your own.

Socially, I would involve myself in the leadership of various societies and events, in order to gain the skills and competencies I needed to kick-start my career. My involvement with a society aimed at Black students on campus would stir up a lifelong commitment to working towards increasing meaningful diversity and broadening access. My position meant other students would often confide in me, with hope that the society might be able to help in some way. In truth, I was less surprised by the casual acts of silent discrimination we had all experienced: from comments about the structure of Black families to the stereotypical notions of how we dressed and talked, we all had, in some way shape or form, experienced the same thing. What was more surprising, was the identical nature of the incidents we had experienced. From police searches to 'playground banter', we had all, one way or another, experienced the same thing. And whilst we laughed and joked our way through such stories, the negative impacts they had had were so plain and obvious. Black boys are too often the target of needless criticism and the subject of harsh criticism. Over the course of three years, I would be stopped by the police over seven times, each in different locations, but with the same excuses: matched identities, 'increased gang activity in the area', or 'you looked suspicious'. The impact of such occurrences has a profound effect on so many people, and we must all do more to acknowledge it and work towards eliminating it.

We had all, in one way or another, been reminded – whether by parents or senior relatives – of the colour of our skin and the world in which we lived. From suggestions of tailoring speeches to advice on what to wear, each of us had encountered advice which whilst coming from a place of love and caution, revealed the sad nature of the society we lived in.

Over the course of university, and through my involvement with the society, I would become acutely aware of the challenges we face, and also, the possible solutions we could all use to change our institutions. I would engage in several conversations with senior members of staff about the changes that had to be made and the things the university needed to do better. Throughout all these, one example has and will always stand out: a very senior member of staff, who was White, would invite me into his office. "Jeff," he said, "I need your help." He would openly and honestly admit that we had a problem that needed to be solved. For a senior member of staff, his humility and honesty would allow me to open up and offer ideas – and his position and experience would give him the platform to mentor me. With his help, support and influence, the society would go on to create events, offer meaningful careers advice and help Black students establish events and programmes that were for them. We hosted dinners and events where Black members of staff reminisced about their experiences and gave some helpful advice, and students would proudly display their culture and interests with their attires and accessories. All of that came from an honest and open conversation where two people, with different experiences, sought to come up with a way to shape their institution for the better. As a result, we were to win an award for the 'Best New Society' in the country. Our mentoring scheme, which paired Black students with Black professionals did well to help increase confidence and raise aspirations. After graduating and at the height of the Black Lives Matter protest following the death of George Floyd, he (the White senior member of staff) would send a message that once again revealed his acknowledgement of the problem and reaffirmed his commitment to help change it.

I am not suggesting that praise be poured on people for simply acknowledging a problem exists, but I do think credit should be given when people in positions of responsibility admit, with open humility and confidence, that there is a problem. And even more importantly, work with people affected, to try and take meaningful steps to solve that problem.

But for continued progress, especially after the Black Lives Matter Protests and the death of George Floyd, everyone − from educational institutions and corporations to government bodies − should view diversity, inclusion and representation not as an act of isolated charity or a means to polish their external images, but as an essential part of improving society and increasing access for all.

A young Black boy or girl, who might be busy worrying about which cartoon to watch right now, should not have to rely, as I did, on their Black teachers or lecturers for targeted support or mentoring. Rather, they should expect and demand that their institutions and organisations they belong to or aspire to be part of, work tirelessly, regardless of the race of their leadership, to improve access for all.

Obed Adomako

I want to simply impact the lives of others to fulfil their purpose in life. Overall, sharing my story reminded me to not be complacent in the position that I am in now but to strive for more. I am forever grateful for the opportunity to share my experience but also to unlock some doors that had been locked and forgotten about, but worth exposing. Not only did I share this chapter out of my own interest but to also impact you as the reader.

Soar Higher

Can I be real with you here in this chapter; honest and vulnerable as much as I can?
Thank you.

I guess you might be impressed with my various little accomplishments but that's not why we are both here. Accolades and achievements can only impress someone but not cause an impact. We as humans are shaped by the lessons we encounter on our path and I believe a lesson learned should be a lesson shared. Life in itself requires us to take control of it rather than controlling us. My desire at the end is to drop my pen knowing you will close this chapter with a tremendous zeal to not only take a step to write your own script but cause a change in your life and your current surrounding.

First of five children born to young migrant workers who struggled to make ends meet but in God's own will, their paths of sweat and pain were knitted together in Italy for a purpose. My childhood was a blessing in disguise; being diagnosed with a weak immune system and developmental stammering among a few others not to mention of, set the perfect battle scene. Lesson 1: the toughest mountains are given to those capable to climb, meaning you are more than gifted to reach the apex. A two-year-old me found myself in Africa, in the arms of my grandmother whom I owe everything, because of the several home evictions and life-threatening accidents my parents had to endure to put something on the table every evening. Things got from bad to worse when my grandmother passed away shortly after which left me without a relative to turn to. At that tender age, I got the opportunity of a lifetime to experience the two extremities in our current society: the lifestyle of the rich and the poor. The standard of living in some of these areas gave me a different perspective in life to not only work hard but lend a hand one day to the less privileged. Fast forward a few months, was brought back to Italy and found myself starting school at the age of four completely new to a different culture which required me to adapt.

Lesson 2: adapt to survive. If there was a word I could sign as mine in the dictionary, it would be adaptation. For years science even believes we are a species adapted to the demands of this earth for our survival. Within a short period of time, I had to learn a new language, culture whilst also making friends. If you do not remember anything from this chapter, please write down the word adapt somewhere. Regardless of the situation or the change in circumstances, those who thrive are always the ones who can adapt quickly stemming a reaction which influences the outcome positively in most cases.

As I went through the new educational system I was introduced to smoothly simply by adapting to suit the requirements of the culture and its people. Made a lot of childhood friends and memories which brings a smile when replaying it in my head. But, it was not all glittering all the time, dream crushers and being looked past were some battles I got to fight earlier than I expected. I only realised it a few years ago that I was only welcomed during our PE lessons hence my endless love for fitness because that was where I found my voice through my abilities. Being stripped of your humanity can be a hard pill to swallow for anyone, even more so for a schoolboy and recently found the root of my imposter syndrome emotions in certain settings. This together with my stammering issues resulted me hiding in my own shell. I only felt comfortable to express myself by either running the quickest and jumping the highest just to feel embraced. This is a continuous trend within my cultures and is engraved in our brains to always outwork our white counterparts. Obviously to everything there is positives and negatives and having this mindset weighed extremely heavy on me. There has always been a stigma especially on young men to deal with our struggles in silence and not showing any sign of weakness. For years we have been educated by both society and family to suppress any feelings, but fortunately we are on the right trajectory to raise more awareness on mental health in the male population. Only learned that vulnerability is a super-power that only the brave can expose their challenges and seek help to improve on them. I went through the struggles to adapt and the feeling of not being accepted alone without reaching out. For anyone who can relate, I want to encourage you that speaking up and asking for help is absolutely fine. To become a better version of yourself requires you to prune away and unlearn some behaviours that influences our actions and sharing your emotions is one.

Venturing into an unknown territory can be very daunting at first and that was the exact thing I felt when I decided to open up. Changing a habit that has been engraved in our heads, will take time and that is absolutely fine. You should not feel there has not been any progress so it is a failure. Even the thought of seeking for help is a massive step itself. Try eliminating any judgemental thoughts and be the one to break any stereotype. You might be wondering how do I get rid of something that forms part of my identity? Take heart, first of all our identity is in constant evolution with our existence; my thought process and perspective on life is completely different to 2–3 years ago. There is no harm in letting go something to make room for a new thing. If doesn't work out, there is always a 9/10 chance to go back. There is satisfaction in trying than living in regret. And finally, be particular about what you feed on and here is another area of particular interest. I can dive into a whole different dimension on the importance and effect of what we feed our brains and bodies. Personally, nutrition also encompasses what we read and listen. I will be completely honest with you all, I have noticed a significant change ever since I stopped following some Instagram pages and listening to certain types of music which encourages the wrong definition of an alpha mentality.

Moving on, I was soon again sent back to Africa which was when I became deeply appreciative of the life I was living in Italy even though

I had my own struggles I was dealing with. Here again, someone might argue I might feel at home on my own land and living among my people but that was not the case. Was left out on many occasions since they thought I couldn't relate to their living conditions simply due to the fact I didn't grow up there. It required time and effort to adapt and blend myself in with them making it difficult to leave when the time was due to come into the UK. My few years here has not been a smooth sail. Am currently working as a cleaner as well as doing my degree, leading a Christian society on campus and also being a BAME advocate. Why did I choose to take up all of these opportunities? To simply give you a glimpse of hope that everything is possible. All the experiences in Africa, racism at a young age and being told I was not in the position to make my dreams a reality were just obstacles I needed to hurdle over. It is vital we don't stop at the hurdle but adapt to jump over.

Not sure where to draw the line here, but can I leave you with a secret with the example of an eagle? I had to go through a process of change early last year where I put on myself to erase any past memories, break certain stereotypes, words that discouraged me and even distance myself from certain environments. Isolated from the negativity and other external pressures, I indulged and invested into getting to know who I am and educating myself on certain areas of weakness. This principle was adopted through learning the rebirth of an eagle which occurs after it's lived for 40 years. It hides itself on the peak of a mountain and endures a gruesome experience of plucking it out its beak, talons and feathers to soar higher. Take some time out during these quarantining days to explore more of who you are and where you want to get in the near future. Your future and life in general, is what you make it.

I hope I painted a picture in your head making your dreams seem more obtainable. Remember that even though challenges may come, you will tell your story one day. Adapt to your current situation and give your maximum effort regardless.

You are the main character of your story.

Foridha Ahmed

Sharing my story in this book has made me appreciate how far I have come and how much I've learned, and in the future, I hope to continue to acknowledge the progress I have made professionally and personally. I hope to make people feel comfort/get advice relating to the struggles of mental health as a student and once teenager.

Dealing with mental health – a hopeful perspective backstory

As I sit cross-legged on the cold winter night, I reminisce the feelings of 2020. In 20 years of living, I feel almost at my worst, trapped in purgatory. A feeling of uncertainness, and a slow steady pain that burns around my edges like a candle flame against the wax.

Then I remember the feeling of cold against my skin, that feels
strangely comforting.
An introduction to where I am now:
The rain drizzles against the worn-out concrete pavement
An icy winter breeze that catches your breath
Yet it leaves a warm aftertaste on your lips
The subdued orange hue fizzles out into the early night
With nothing but the moon as your company
The night is silent from man, but their presence lingers
As the radio chatter and vivid lights bring houses to life
The icy breeze now kisses your skin tenderly
And brings your body warmth in an unusual way
An eerie silence falls, yet static has never felt so welcoming

© Foridha Ahmed, 2020

I hope these words bring comfort as they do to me. I wrote this poem because winter can be lonely, bleak and dark, especially now. Yet the forgiving nature of winter allows you to feel these emotions void of guilt and brings a strange unexplainable comfort as it validates the way you feel.

I have had my fair share of downfalls, as I am sure many of us have had. For me, it had to do with the taboo world of mental health. It can feel like you are the only one struggling at times, and that is why I was encouraged to share this, to hopefully bring others comfort in reading this and direction.

Many of us have faced challenges, instead of delving into mine in great depth I wish for you to interpret the broadness of the way I write against *your* challenges. My hope for this is that it brings comfort, you can better deal with your emotions and are hopeful of the future.

Challenges

A sinking feeling is one that holds me tightly, and hopefulness of life to move in a different direction is a way that I have felt for a few years, scattered between beautiful fragments of happiness.

Life had led me up to the main event, an experience that left me feeling rather knocked down and gifted me a fresh pair of lenses.

Truths

Therapy is normal. For many years I had thought of Therapy as a last resort and often demonised it. Until I had learned of people around me that had sought these services in the past; an experience that stands out in my memory, was someone I had known neither well nor long, mentioning their Therapy unsolicited. Finally, elated at the fact that Therapy is normal and accepted. Free services such as Healthy Minds offer CBT, which depends on the individual's capacity to change their perceptions and practice lifelong coping skills.

Speak your feelings. Being able to uncover the hurt you feel with a trusted person is a gift and a weight off your shoulders. Samaritans is a charity that offers a 24-hour helpline on 116 123 that will give an ear to listen.

Embrace gratitude. Often heard, but not commonly practised. True happiness lies in gratefulness, trusting the process as time is a healer and, in the meantime, embrace the present.

The key to happiness

Many of us are often bothered by sleepless nights; thoughts of what may the future have in store for us. What goal are you striving towards reaching? I can tell you sanity has to be sought in reality. We cannot spend our days lingering in uncertainty, but we can change our mentality towards the future.

Striking me one afternoon, shrivelled up in my PJs and greasy bed hair; I had suddenly possessed the key to contentment in a conveniently placed article. "Woman, 90, dies giving up ventilator saying...," the notification had read. Immediately clicking on it, my interest peaked amidst the growing pandemic scares. I did not know that what would follow would lead me to indulge in the most fulfilling week ahead. The article read "...save it for the younger patients. I already had a good life." My condolences are with the family of Suzanne Hoylaerts, though the world had not borne a soul lost, but rather witnessed a celebration of a long life, filled with beautiful moments. A life I wish for everyone to able to experience – she is indeed a hero. And this very thinking helped me to see the silver lining amidst a thunderstorm.

Many of us are accustomed to shrouding our thinking with negativity at times of hardship. It is okay to feel downfalls, but it is important to not let this feeling linger. The days, months and possibly years we may surrender to this build-up of feelings, when no one wants to look back on wasted time.

Accepting our situation as it is, without diminishing the hardship anyone is facing, and practising gratitude for what we have is the key to happiness. A past self would disregard this as nonsensical, yet that outlook left me feeling bleak. I know many of us have been there, and hope lies in the perspective we nurture.

I had accepted where I was and focused on the present. A nourishing feeling of contentment and peace fuelled my week, and I felt happy. Nothing could take away from it as I did not allow it.

Not attempting to paint the perfect picture, as I have fallen into negative thinking since then, but I always come out of it. Remember that it is okay to feel blue, but do not let it consume you and waste any more of your precious time.

I hope that this chapter was even the slightest enlightening. And I wish you the best for the future.
Take care.

Chloe Ambrose

The world has already changed so much since my teenage years. For that, I am incredibly grateful that the next generation may feel more accepted for what they look like, where they are from, what they want to wear and what they want to do in life. I hope my story provides insight for the next generation who have no choice but to heal from what has already happened and rebuild with the knowledge that positive change is happening.

Embrace you even when others do not

Our differences can sometimes pose as the keys to other people's locked-door beliefs. Your confidence at school kept the bully's self-doubt turning. Your clear complexion revealed your co-worker's mad skin insecurities. Your new sports car unearthed the neighbour's deepest desires sparking jealous aspiration. Your pursuit for the dream life meant the boyfriend waking up from a nightmare where he's not in it.

As we're all coming to learn, our quirks can be another's downfall, and that what people project onto us is often a reflection of how they feel about themselves. I think I knew this from a very young age but they weren't words anyone used back then. At school I would hold on to my mum's excuses that the bully 'was jealous' and 'what goes around comes around'. I'd think this when my hat was stolen and chucked into the tree or 'ginger, ginger' shouted at me from down the hall. I actually remember my child mind finding it really silly that I was being picked on for my hair. It just didn't make sense to me. And, I'm glad it didn't make sense because without that perspective and intuition, that my hair colour wasn't in fact causing any real problem to other people's lives, I probably wouldn't have gone back into school each and every day. Rising above the hate, I pressed on. Embracing me.

A life lesson, haters don't stop at school; they follow you into adulthood too. Joy. Besides, I remember hearing a quote once that said if you had haters then you're doing something right. This was my first bit of proof that the haters didn't dislike me for me, they disliked me for the parts of me they didn't have.

My adult experience of this was regrettably during university where I quickly realised that university was not going to be what I thought it would be. My perception of leaving home for further education included thoughts of finally finding people that had the same amount of eagerness and passion as I. Most people I talked to were overwhelmed by the girl with all the ideas, the girl who wanted to take the harder route to stand out and, subsequently, get us all a better grade.

That's the thing, from a young age I always thought in a different way, choosing to put my work together to impress a parent, teacher, examiner, making them sit up and think 'ah, that's a unique perspective' because that would probably result in a higher grade, from not doing what everyone else is doing. I always wanted to embrace my differences because being different meant I was special and that gave me the confidence to push through the frequent lows I found myself in.

And, so, my next three years were a mixture of my eager self putting my hand up in lectures/class and being hated-on because of that. Where people said 'impossible' I said 'possible' – designing, creating, thinking and pushing for the best outcome for our projects. Outside of class, I also refused to follow suit, choosing to wear flats when everyone insisted heels and not going out when everyone demanded I did. Not following the crowd won't get you a large group of friends, I learned, but it did mean I stayed true to myself. I was happier that way, just doing me. However, not everyone wanted to embrace my eager quirks. Once, at university, my lecturer even took me aside and told me I needed to be less excitable in class, you know, be a part of the pack and not be so forthcoming with ideas and opinions. It's easier to silence the one than reason with the many I guess.

None of it made much mental sense to me at university and it was here when I developed an overactive mind that spoke self-critically and made me socially awkward. The internal monologue would say things like 'they hate you' or 'I bet they think that about you' – I even found it hard to look people in the eye, never present in the moment and entirely present in my head. So, I started declining invitations, choosing to focus on my degree and a few friends I did feel comfortable with until I came to a realisation… If I'm going to make it in the media industry I can't keep having my negative self-talk rabbiting away in my head. Somehow, I knew my anxiety didn't have to define me, be me, I knew one way or another I could get rid of it. After all, it was THE main thing holding me back from being the confident person I knew I could be.

Now, this is not me putting you off university, I gained so much perspective and experience at university, connections too. One connection of mine is now even a paying client. What I want you to know is that people will be around you wherever you go. Some may like you, some may not, you can't get everyone to like you and neither will you like everyone. These factors around us we can't control. Yes, we can choose who we're friends with and who we avoid but we'll never be able to control another's mind. So, the next best thing is for us to control our own. At some point in your life you may also come to a realisation, this may come to you via your gut instinct, intuition, that a better you/a more fulfilling life lies on the other side of an obstacle. Here's my take on approaching the obstacle of anxiety.

Overcoming obstacles can be tricky when your world views something as perfectly normal. Negative self-talk, for example, my parents stressed, was one of those things 'we all do' and is therefore 'normal'. In these moments, where your gut instinct meets another person's belief, you may have to swerve around them and keep pressing on, without their support or understanding. That's hard. Having your parents label you 'fine' when you're telling them you're struggling was one of the biggest challenges and potential setbacks I had to face. It was my first realisation that your parents don't always know what's best for you. That, actually, they can be the core catalyst of obstacles, forever keeping you 'safe' for what could happen as opposed to what could be. Wasting my money on seeking help was one of their beliefs, I saw it as investment, they did not. Taking my only £600 left after my years at university, I sought a thrive therapist. This was the first positive step of many I would take for myself and by myself.

The perception of doing things for ourselves is changing. There are less jibes of selfishness and more words encouraging the practice of self-love. Hallelujah! But your journey to becoming your own mentor, fitness coach, therapist, parent, lover and friend, may only just be beginning. If so, what I would encourage you to do, from my own experience, is to truly feel and seek answers from within yourself. Knowing the difference between intuition and mental natter is so important because it's your body's way of saying... positive change needs to happen.

So, if any part of your world doesn't sit right to you, be it that friend who always puts you down, the lover that isn't meeting your basic needs, the job that forces you into a box, the lack of adventures you've always yearned for, make the vow to yourself to do something about it. Carry yourself through and past other people's expectations and make a plan to welcome positive change into your life. When you feel the warm sensation of your own hand intertwined with yourself, leading you the way you've always dreamed of, you'll realise that there is everything you could want for yourself with a little self-love and self-courage.

Looking back now, I'm grateful for my journey. Now, I'm surrounded by some of the best people who accept me for me, the quirky ball of ginger energy that I've always been. It's strange, it's almost as if I've only been living my true authentic self these last few years. Before, I would always choose to hide or dilute my personality for others, for fear of not being liked. But, I can confidently say I don't do that anymore. I accept me and that's all that matters.

I'll leave you with my biggest learning. The only person you can truly rely on, when no one else is around, is you. You can choose to get sucked in to other people's insecurities or life's setbacks or you can continue to do you. To live life the way you want to positively live it. No valentines? Write yourself a card. No travel-loving relatives? Go on a solo adventure. No friends? Be your own friend. In these actions, lie the realisation that we are never really alone when we befriend and embrace ourselves.

Mohammed Abbas Aslam

My hope for the future is for there to be equal opportunities for all, and that no one is judged on their heritage and race. Sharing my story has enabled me to reflect on my journey of how I have gotten to where I am today and has served as motivation on why I am pursuing my goals. I personally want to help others through my story and tell you that it is never too late to reach your goals and to be proud of what you have achieved so far and to create positives from negatives.

Be proud of who you are and what you have achieved

When I was growing up, I would hear adults talking about how difficult life is when you are older. But why wasn't life acknowledged as difficult for children too? Growing up, I faced so many struggles, both inside and outside of school. Throughout my academic life, I faced both racism and bullying. I was met with premature judgement due to my socio-economic class and the area from which I reside. For example, in school, I was labelled as the kid from the "druggie" area. Honestly speaking, it was so hard for me to ignore the comments at the time, but I am now stronger and will not let anybody make me feel less of myself.

I reside from a background whereby both of my parents never attended university. One of my parents opted for the Youth Training Scheme (YTS) and the other worked a low-income job. My parents have always been supportive of my academic journey and have always pushed me to do my very best. Although we were a low-income family, they made so many sacrifices so that I could have the opportunity to attend tutor classes. This is what drove me to focus on education, as I wanted to make them proud and show that their efforts and sacrifices for my education really paid off. Although my tutor classes ended as I began secondary school, I had to browse for resources online to review past papers and revision materials in order to achieve the grades I was aspiring for. I was at a disadvantage compared to other students as I could not have private tutoring to help me with the subjects that I was weak at. But that is what drove me to achieve what I currently have. In the end, I managed to exceed the grades I was hoping for and this was down to my own initiative by studying constantly at home and at school. The lesson I have learned was not to dwell on what I do not have but make do with the resources I do have as there are other people in far worse situations than me and have made something of themselves due to their own initiative.

When I started secondary school, I felt out of place due to being a BAME (Black, Asian and Minority Ethnic) student. During my time there, I had experienced a lot of racism. Students would joke about my name as it is a commonly used Muslim name 'Mohammed'. This was so upsetting for me as the name 'Mohammed' is special for Muslims. I began to feel embarrassed about my name and because the racism would not stop, it came to a point where I wanted to change my name. I also faced comments made about us minority people taking all the jobs and we should 'go back to where we came from'. This upset me a lot as the minorities helped this country and our ancestors moved to this country to provide their families with a better future. Contrary to this, I was also bullied for my weight. This made me feel self-conscious and I did not feel comfortable around people. Because the bullying was not being dealt with, I decided to move to another school. Moving schools was the best decision I had ever made. My new school had students from a variety of nationalities. I felt more comfortable as I was not the odd one out from an ethnic minority. Furthermore, my new school did not tolerate bullying and racism which made me feel safer and happier. However, there was a time when terrorist attacks were taking place frequently around the world. This caused my peers to make rude comments about my religion and after that I felt everything had changed. People's opinions started to change, and the comments became racist and hurtful. Going through all of this, I realised how common bullying is. My advice for anybody who is being bullied is to report it. You do not deserve to be bullied and you have the right to be happy.

After finishing secondary school and achieving my grades that I had aspired for, it was important for me to look for a part-time job whilst studying in sixth form. This part-time job would allow me to support myself and take some financial pressure off my parents. It was really difficult for me to secure a job. I faced a lot of rejection emails. Personally, I feel like there needs to be more guidance in schools for job hunting. Maybe workshops like writing a CV and job interview skills would be useful. This would allow students to gain knowledge on what employers are looking for and how to conduct themselves when being interviewed. Due to my struggles of not being able to secure a part-time job, I became demotivated and did not take job hunting seriously anymore. Eventually I did land myself a part-time job – perseverance is key.

After completing sixth form, I applied for an apprenticeship in Birmingham as I thought I would not be able to achieve the grades required for the course I wanted to study in university. The apprenticeship requirement was five GCSEs, which I had already achieved. I got the position and worked at the establishment for a month until A-level results day. To my surprise, I had achieved the grades required and had secured a place in my first-choice university. I now had two choices: continue with the apprenticeship or go to university. I felt like I was stuck in a dilemma. So, I thought about the positives and negatives of continuing with the apprenticeship. I had decided to go to university as I had worked hard in sixth form to secure a place. I also wanted to make my parents proud as they had tried their best to motivate me with my education. The lesson that I had learned was always think positively and not to underestimate my capabilities.

During my time at university, I have become a more confident person. Teamwork has helped me with my confidence as my course requires us to team up and work on projects with students from other courses. Before university, I was anxious about meeting new people but now I have worked with several new faces in group projects and have even become friends with my peers. This is beneficial for when I land a graduate job as I will be communicating with new colleagues. Furthermore, my presentation skills have improved massively. At the end of the group projects, we are required to present the product produced in front of the lecturers. During my first presentation I felt nervous and I did not know how to present myself. However, through practice, I can now present in front of an audience, I can keep them engaged and I know what is expected of me. My advice to gain confidence is by putting yourself in situations where you are not usually comfortable. Try something new. Another tip is to ask for feedback. This way you know what to improve on in the future.

I have enjoyed my time at university and have been happy with the help that is provided to me to secure a graduate job. The Careers team have been very helpful with improving my LinkedIn profile and my CV. Although this past year has been very tough for me and for everyone else as the pandemic has essentially brought most things to a halt, I am remaining hopeful. My final year curriculum is mainly online, and this has not been beneficial as I feel like I do not have the facilities to study well. I am however making the most of what I can and am trying my best to keep positive during this uncertain time. Furthermore, I miss the social aspect of university where I used to see my peers almost every day. To overcome this, we now speak regularly over the phone.

To conclude, I am proud of my background and where I came from to what the future beholds. I am proud of my name, and my culture. I also have learned to not underestimate my capabilities and not sell myself short as I will never gain the opportunities I have now if I always think that I would not be able to succeed. Currently, I am completing my final year of university and am ready to embark on my journey of securing a graduate job. I have remained positive during this pandemic and I would like to make my parents proud during this unprecedented time. My hope for the future is for BAME individuals to have equal opportunities and not be judged on their heritage and race. The chapter has enabled me to reflect on my journey to reach where I am today and has served as motivation on why I am pursuing my goals. I personally want to help others by reaching people through my story and tell them it is never too late to reach their goals and to be proud of what they have achieved so far and to create positives from negatives.

Shanique Clarke

I hope that whatever I do in the future, I help others along the journey to understand that you can reach any height you wish with hard work and belief in yourself. Sharing my story in the book was quite emotional and helped me to realise how far I have come and how much further I've got to go! It is only the start of my journey.

It's not rejection, it's redirection

To anyone who has ever doubted themselves. This is for you.

Although being Mancunian has shaped who I am today, it wouldn't be without my Jamaican heritage that has added the finer details to my character. 'Likkle but tallawah' is a saying that I, like many other Jamaican descendants, grew up with. Used in Jamaica to describe how although a small island, Jamaica is still mighty in power and strength, is a sentiment I have carried with me throughout my 23 years so far. That wasn't the only proverb I was brought up on. 'Patient man ride donkey' is another Jamaican phrase which rings true. This saying speaks directly to the art of patience. Sister to 'patience is a virtue', 'patient man ride donkey' means that if you're ambitious and want to reach a particular height, you need to get there without cutting corners (even if that means taking the long way around). Once you reach your destination, you can be at peace knowing you don't have to turn back, and you haven't compromised yourself. Yet, whilst I had these words of affirmation stuck in my head, I still found myself questioning my abilities.

I think doubting yourself comes in seasons. Some seasons are yours, you're on a winning streak, the road to success. Whereas in other seasons it may feel like you are on a long road scattered with hurdles. My educational journey has been a bit like that. A story of the highest highs (and some of my proudest moments) but also some of my more sombre times filled with disappointment and disillusionment. Regardless of where I am in my journey, I have always remembered that this is not my final form, nor my final outcome. A negative situation can turn into a positive and even amazing accomplishment in an instant.

I believe that life is all about defining moments. A set of experiences and life conditions which make you, you. These don't always have to be big life-altering events. Even the littlest thing can have the biggest impact, shaping who you are forever.

Looking back at my educational experiences, I always felt shy. I was the student in the classroom who found it difficult to answer a question out of fear of getting it wrong. Or avoided putting myself out there because I was anxious what other people would think of me.

I spent much of my high school years attempting to fit in. Like many who attend an all-girls school, I tried so hard to have the right hair, wear the right clothes and be someone that everyone liked. Looking back, I was never going to fit in, I was one of few who looked very different to the majority. This only left me confused about who I was and began my journey of imposter syndrome. Imposter syndrome is the buzz word of the past few years but perfectly encapsulates how many of us feel. Imposter syndrome is a state of mind where you doubt your skills, talents and achievements. I think it's very normal for people to be unsure of themselves at certain times in their lives.

It's safe to say I've always ranked myself as below average when it comes to academic ability. In high school, I was always in the second set and felt that I had to work extra hard to get average grades. They say that comparison is the thief of joy. Together with doubting my ability, I started to believe that I was not 'smart', even though my ambitions were sky high.

When I was in year nine, I experienced my first real taste of failure. This was a defining moment for me, as it impacted how I would approach education for many years to come. Back then, my year group was part of a guinea pig trial where year nines sat a GCSE option in a single

31

year. Maybe this was a disaster waiting to happen. After studying the course content for the year, I remember feeling confident that I had put my all into the exam. As I opened the results, the realisation sunk in that I had in fact failed my GCSE Spanish exam. I'll always remember that day because of the number of tears I shed. I felt so embarrassed but most importantly disappointed in myself. Luckily for me, in true helicopter mom style, my mum swooped in and before I knew it was resitting the exam. As a know-it-all 14-year-old, I thought she was being dramatic and kicking up a fuss. After all, I was the only student in the class who chose to re-sit an exam from the year before. Now, as I look back, I am so appreciative that she forced me to try again and achieve a better grade.

A few years later, when sitting my A levels at college, the second defining moment hit me. When I think back to studying for my A levels, all I can think of is how it was the most difficult thing I've ever done. I had my heart set on my first-choice university, and I knew nothing could come between that. Having already experienced my first taste of disappointment, I wasn't in a rush to experience round two. I worked so hard, sacrificing short-term enjoyment for long-term victory. Of course, when A-level results day came, I was tossing and turning all night. The sinking feeling I felt deep in my chest is one I will never forget. My world felt like it was falling apart. The excitement I should have felt for doing well in two of my subjects was clouded by the disappointment in the final grade of another. Without checking whether my first-choice university had accepted me, I rang the clearing hotline in tears, begging to be accepted onto any course at my star university. To my surprise, I had been accepted onto my chosen course and soon enough the tears of disappointment turned to tears of joy.

When starting out at university, my fear was that my A levels might be a hindrance in my future job search. This case of imposter syndrome fuelled my 'do everything you can' attitude to strengthen my employability. Fully immersing myself into the university experience, I participated in anything and everything from ambassador posts, mentorships, placement years, society memberships and part-time work. I worked hard throughout my four years at university consistently achieving a 2:1. Although I dreamt and hoped I would finish university with a first-class degree, I never believed that I was smart enough to achieve the coveted grade. Completing my final year exams and dissertation within a pandemic was so difficult however I persevered and continued to push on. Whilst my story is not yet over, I can proudly say that after years of doubting myself, I finally proved myself wrong and achieved a first-class honours degree!

The year 2020 is a memorable one. For many it will be memories of a pandemic and pandemonium. For me, the theme of this year is resilience. When coupled with hard work and perseverance, resilience often is met with success and achievement. But one thing I have learned is that success doesn't always look how you imagine it. For me, success was securing a graduate job, getting my driving licence and finally beginning my 'adult' life. However, the pandemic had other plans.

There's been so many things this year that I never thought would have happened and so many more things I had expected to achieve.

I never thought my academic journey would continue after my four years of undergraduate study. And maybe if there wasn't a pandemic and the jobs market hadn't been affected, I would have got a job and progressed the way I envisioned. Just because these things didn't happen doesn't mean I'm a failure.

Being a student is a huge part of our lives. From aged four to twenty-something (and even older), education has played an enormous part in figuring out who we are. In this realm, success is confined by certificates, grade boundaries and acceptance emails. Over time, you can dwell on when you don't achieve your targets. It's so easy to forget and gloss over your little wins. Sometimes it can feel like 1 − failure, 0 − you. But remember, that each win adds to your overall score book. Never forget to account for ALL your wins because they will always stack up against any disappointments.

For me, the past five years are a testament of grit and resilience. From narrowly missing out on my desired A-level grades to achieving a first-class honours degree, I have proved that I can achieve, and I am determined to continue to do so. So, take it from me; praise each success, learn from every disappointment and keep striving forward. It can feel like a rejection, but you're being redirected to something better.

Cody Croxall

Sharing my story, has allowed me to reflect on my journey and see that there were ups and downs that I have been able to overcome and that have helped me grow. I hope that this helps others to feel inspired when they feel like they cannot do something and have that self-belief and confidence in their abilities.

River of Life – My life lessons

So here goes with my river of life. With life things don't always go right and the way you want them to and I accepted that from a young age. I was told by my English teacher when I was in year 7 that I wouldn't pass my English GCSE. As you can imagine this wasn't nice to hear at all, but instead of letting it upset me I made it motivate me. I've always been someone who loves proving people wrong and I did. I guess that was one of my first key lessons in life **"Don't believe everything people tell you."**

High school isn't the easiest time for anyone, people try to get you down and do it to protect their own reputation. It's very much a 'dog eat dog world' where you have to be the strongest dog in the pack to come out at the top. Just remember that you are never alone in that period and there are people to talk to if you need. There were some days for myself where it felt like hell, I was enthusiastic when it came to learning and tried to make it enjoyable, this wasn't always the most popular way, but you know it's all about me proving people wrong. I didn't let them get me down, I kept going and used music as a way to zone out. This way I wouldn't let it affect me or my education at that stage. I learned through that period of time that **"Not everyone wants the best for you"**, it's all about keeping those people that do close to you and never taking that for granted.

34

Through the highs and lows of high school my confidence took a hit but my high school journey did end on quite a high, I went to prom which was something, for the first four years, I doubted I would do but I did. I walked in that room with my head held high and that felt like I'd finally won, I'd proven people wrong. I got my results which I was pleased with and my parents were also overjoyed and celebrated them with me. I remember seeing the 'B' next to the English ones and thinking "Yes, I did it". That was a defining moment of my life **"For others to believe in you, you have to believe in yourself."** That's my biggest tip for anyone.

I went to a college that hardly anyone from my high school went to. I wanted a challenge. I'm very much a person who seeks challenges to push myself. This year was one of the toughest in my life, I didn't fit in, I didn't make many friends at that point and I failed, I didn't pass college and I thought that my time in education was up. This decision could have defined me. I spoke to my parents and gave myself a pep talk and said, "I prove people wrong so it's time to prove myself wrong for the first time." I lost my confidence, I knew I needed to make a change and that's when I decided to move college and give it one last go, I remember saying "Cody, you've got this" and that's when I learned **"Never give up."** So the next chapter of my life began.

My second go at college wasn't as straightforward as I hoped, the first year was good, I met friends and did relatively well and got the grades I needed to pass to the second year. I thought "hey I've already beaten my last attempt". I was going in the right direction, but life isn't that simple, it throws things at you when you least expect it to. My second year began, my best friend in my first year of college left, I tried to not let that bother me, I made friends with another group of girls. Things went well until a moment of my life I could never prepare myself for happened. It broke me at the time, my Nan passed away, it shattered me and that taught me to **"Be prepared for the unexpected."** I tried to not let it get me down at the time. The girls I thought were my friends weren't the most supportive so I had to find the courage in myself to carry on. I said to myself "I'm doing it for her, I'm going to do this for my Nan". My final six months at college weren't the easiest. I felt isolated a lot of the time but I used this as a way of doing all my revision at college so my home time was my own time. I guess that's when I learned that, **"through every negative situation something positive can come of it."** I kept my head down and got on with my education whilst always remembering why I wanted to do it.

I did my exams and waited for what seemed like forever to see if I secured my place at university doing a Mathematics teaching degree. Results day came and my dreams shattered – I didn't get what I needed to get on to that course, I always wanted to be a Maths teacher when I was younger, but with determination I was sure that I wouldn't let my dream of getting to university not come true. That's when I learned that, **"failed dreams can make new better dreams happen."** I got offered a few places at university, including Sheffield Hallam, where I wanted to go in the first place so that was that I began my journey at university doing an Accounting and Finance degree.

Once getting to university and starting I questioned if I belonged there to begin with but within time as my confidence grew and I was putting myself forward for extra stuff such as being a course representative. That's when I learned that **"you can help yourself stand out by going the extra mile"**. I did this in my second year and I felt so happy and a sense of belonging for the first time and that's when my life came to a halt when my granddad passed away. Just as I did with my Nan, I knew I had to do it for him. My placement year was full of challenges, but I learned that, **"what doesn't challenge you won't change you."** In that time, I learned how to be a professional and work in an office environment at an amazing company, Rolls-Royce. I came back to university with a new-found confidence and purpose. I was a go-getter, I wanted to do well but this time I was more disciplined with my time management which I learned via work. My final year went well until the global pandemic known as COVID-19 hit us. I adapted to a new way of working and felt more determined then ever to do well. I didn't have a job lined up and that worried me but I remembered to never give up. I kept going with both my studies and applying for my dream graduate job, using the time management I had learned previously. I kept going.

Just after I finished my last exam at university I got a call, the night before, asking if I'd like to attend a virtual assessment centre. I attended it, sometimes you have to **"expect the unexpected"**. I enjoyed the assessment centre, it made me realise even more that I wanted the job. A month passed by in which I didn't have much hope and much to keep me busy – we were in a lockdown after all. I got a call, the call I'd been waiting for. Aviva offered me the job as a graduate project manager. I felt overwhelmed with happiness. **"Patience is key"** is the key takeaway I learned.

I was able to enjoy my summer, a bit of respite before the first day of the rest of my working life would begin. I started my life at Aviva virtually which was challenging. I was a people person, I wanted to network but again I adapted and did my best with that, with fantastic help from the inductions we had. Work was amazing, everything I wanted. No two days are the same as a project manager and I loved the challenge that brought with it. An event at work required volunteers, I put my hand up to host an event virtually which over 2,000 people would see live. I was nervous, I was scared but I learned that, **"Don't worry about failures, worry about the chances you miss when you don't even try."** After the event I got a lot of great feedback of how people enjoyed it. In that moment I felt happy and a real sense of achievement. I smiled. I did it. You can do it too!

"Just remember for others to believe in you, you have to believe in yourself." That's my biggest tip for anyone.

Lauren Dennis

I am grateful for being part of something so special – I feel so honoured to be able to share my story. I want people to know that it is okay not to be okay and it is okay to admit it. The first step is to admit it to yourself first, and once you do, it gets easier to share with others. Everyone goes through struggles, so you are not alone, you do not have to be a product of your environment.

This Thing Called Life

A normal kid

Life has always been somewhat difficult for me. I was diagnosed with Sickle Cell Disease from birth so you could say that kind of set the tone for my life before I even started living.

I have a very big family, loads of siblings, all girls only one boy. Despite having older sisters, I didn't feel as connected to them as I did with my big brother. Strange right, normally having older sisters is every girl's dream, not that I didn't enjoy the experience of having sisters, I loved it I wanted to go everywhere with them, but they were much older than me, so it wasn't the same.

My brother was four years old when I entered the world, he was also diagnosed with sickle cell at birth, so I guess this is why I felt more of a bond with him. You could say I am my brother's keeper, even though he is the older one I've always been by his side as a mother would and he's always had my back like a *super* overprotective big brother would. When he was in pain, I would be there helping him get through it as I know what it feels like. There were times where we would be admitted at the same time, my mum by his side and my dad by mine so you can imagine the pressure our parents felt. A part of me felt guilty. You're probably wondering why I'm the baby sister so why did I feel so guilty? Maybe I was made to feel that way, subconsciously... Who knows? The baby of the family felt so old at a young age... I knew I was very different from then, I felt like I had grown up way before my time. Imagine trying to balance school life, being a normal kid whilst feeling abnormal. Now I was the 'lucky' one or, so I was told. I didn't have as many pain crises as my brother did when I was younger, I mean I did but it *wasn't the same as my brother's* even though we have the same illness the only difference was he just felt pain more frequently and more intense than I did which led to a lot of hospital admissions. I would miss out on school because I was up until the early hours of the morning trying to comfort him, or because I stayed in the hospital with him whenever he would need to go. As I said, I never wanted to leave his side. I felt like I had to always be there even if he didn't need me.

People made me feel like this was the least I could do, "He's feeling your pain as well Lauren." I watched the pain he experienced several times a week but me I was *fine* right or so everyone made me feel? I remember praying to God every time he was in pain begging him to take away his pain and put it all on me. Even though I did feel pain every day, maybe not always physically but I did feel it.

I had severe pneumonia at one point. I say severe because I wasn't admitted to the hospital straight away, so it got worse, but I was the strong one so surely my pain wasn't as painful as my brother's, I was the 'normal kid' right? Looking back, I now know this is where it started, I had to be okay even if I really wasn't.

Living a lie
Life after school was harder than I expected. I had two passions – art and maths. I was tempted to go to university to study architecture but my passion for numbers was way bigger, so my mind swiftly changed and was set on becoming a qualified accountant. I'm a Virgo so of course I had everything planned out and organised before I left school. I enrolled in a financial and accounting course at college, some of my friends were going to the same one, everything was sorted. But then everyone was talking about going to the sixth form. There was this whole stigma around colleges vs sixth form, everyone was saying how only the really smart people went to the sixth form. I was baffled, I

thought I knew my path but if I saw myself as smart that's where I should be going right? That's where I was wrong so take it from me "don't follow fashion" as my mum would say. Do what's right for you. I already had my BTEC course waiting for me, the college was closer to my house, but I let other opinions I took on sway me, alter my path. I applied for two of the highest-ranking sixth forms in my city last minute hoping to get in and I did, I got into the higher ranking one actually and I was happy momentarily. I thought I loved school but when I got to sixth form it all changed. I hated it, I don't know if it was the fact that I had or travel nearly two hours on two different jam-packed buses to get there which meant waking up extra early and I wasn't used to that at all. On top of that, I still had to deal with my sickle cell, and I felt like they didn't understand that. I missed out on so much work because I was in pain all the time, I don't know if it was the stress from all the extra effort I had to put in to get to sixth form but something was impacting me, I felt like everyone was judging me. This stopped me from reaching out for help. It's not like everyone knew about my illness I kept it to myself for the most part, but I just felt like I couldn't keep up, so I left, went to college, regretted it, went back and felt the same. I repeated the cycle until I just admitted defeat. Sixth form was just too different, and I didn't like different. I hated still being in a classroom, getting treated like a kid having homework my friends who went to college didn't experience, they had fun whilst I was trying to fit in.

Floating

After leaving sixth form and many college courses after that I just didn't know what to do. I felt like I was floating… My health made it hard for me to commit to a full-time job and my attention span was getting shorter and shorter after the many courses I started and didn't finish. So, I kind of wrapped myself in a bubble. I didn't know what my next step would be, but I knew where I wanted to be, just needed directions and guidance to get there. But I was struggling alone, although I applied to several different apprenticeships, part-time jobs, nothing came through so I was just sat at home all the time which wasn't good because as the 'outcast' I was clashing with everyone or should I say everyone was clashing with me! Why, I don't know, because I was trying so hard to better my position, but no one could see it, they didn't care to ask they just said I wasn't moving. Knowing I wasn't living up to my full potential this made me feel even more down, I was depressed stressed, full of doubt and hopelessness. Full of frustration I was tired. Tired of getting turned down because of not meeting the qualification requirements. But I never stopped applying. That's when I got the breakthrough, I was waiting for my childhood dream job as a receptionist at Ford the car dealership which I visited with my mom and brother the previous year and I fell in love. So, in love that I said to myself when I was there, I'm going to work here one day, and that day came just when I needed it. I was ecstatic, I've always loved admin type work but that didn't last long either. I didn't tell them about my health, I never liked disclosing that I've got sickle cell, I felt like it would hinder my chances but that was silly of me. I ended up getting fired, me calling in sick all the time was an issue and I understood although I did eventually tell them about the pain I go through every day. They still did what they did as I was bad for business, I suppose… I was so embarrassed I didn't tell anyone up until this day, you guys are the first people I'm telling. Remember when I said I had to be okay even if I wasn't. This was one of those moments.

The start of something new

After a rough couple of months, my luck finally started to pick up. I reached out to the social mobility foundation, a charity I connected with whilst I was at sixth form. Hoping they could help me start my career and they did. I was offered a ten-week summer internship at an investment firm called Schroders. The only 'problem' was it was in London. Now I say problem, but it wasn't necessarily a problem for me but others around me. I knew I had to make a decision and quick. I love London so the fact that I would have to move there was exciting for me, I was looking forward to it. But being the baby of the family, everyone made me feel like this was too big of a move. I began to doubt myself even though I knew this was what I was hoping and praying for. "LONDON! Lauren, you can do this in Sheffield, there's no need to move, you're being unrealistic, plus you're needed, you need us, what about your health" all these opinions coming at me, but something in me knew not to listen, not this time anyway. I had to do what was right for me. It was the start of something new and I loved it the whole experience, being in London always made me feel good but this time it was different, I was working there, living the life of a 'Londoner'. Whilst I was there, I felt so alive. I was finally doing me. I wasn't worried about my health I was focused; I saw the bigger picture and this time I saw myself in it.

My life

London gave me a whole new outlook on life. I mean, I always knew what I wanted to do but I felt like it would take me forever to get there due to the fact I left sixth form then college and all my age mates were in their last year of university and I felt extremely behind. Like the snail in the race. But whilst I was in London being around so many talented young professionals I was filled with a different type of drive. I never stopped my apprenticeship search. I was successful in securing three interviews, one at Barclays Bank, Lloyds bank and the other at Coutts. I was so proud of myself. A bank, wow! Me? Lauren! Who's dreamed of working in a bank since a child. Even though they were just interviews, I felt like this was a sign that I am capable, and I should start living my life the way I wanted.

Back to normal

It was nearly the end of my internship I didn't want to leave, and I almost thought I wouldn't. But unfortunately, there wasn't a position available at Schroders, I didn't get the job at Barclays, but I was successful for Lloyds, that was back in Sheffield though and if I was honest, I did not want to go back. I was happy in London; I had a great support system there and I just wasn't ready to leave. I was walking along Waterloo Bridge waiting for a response from Coutts. But it wasn't the news I was hoping for unfortunately, I was unsuccessful. As much as I wanted the apprenticeship, I said to myself it wasn't the right time, but I fell so in love with the bank I kept telling myself I would be back.

Back in Sheffield, I started working at Lloyds Bank and I loved it. I finally got some banking experience I been destined for; I still had my support system by my side, things were great, I was happy. But at the same time, I was getting tired, tired of the same old. I saw what was possible in London and I had to find a way back, but it was hard, the competition in London was something else but I didn't let that demotivate me. I continued applying for everything I saw fit, but my options were minimal. So, until then I played the waiting game.

2020.

What a strange and unexpected year, I know we can all agree on that one. I never saw what this year would bring me. I'm normally so precise in my actions but I also can be very impulsive. Growing up so independent didn't help my situation either. If I could describe myself in three words, affectionate, transparent and emotionally available wouldn't be any of them. I wish but I'm still learning. I wish I could turn back the time, things would be way different. And having the people that are supposed to be there for you no matter what throw certain things in your faces make you question your own actions. But everyone makes mistakes I guess; the most important thing is how you apply your learning from them mistakes. I'm still applying so I don't have much to say in 2020. But I would say please don't feel like you have to take on the world by yourself because I did that, and I'm still paying for it. Also be disciplined about what you respond and react to. Not everyone deserves your time, energy and attention even if its family. Stay in your light, peace of mind is the real bag, and you have to protect it at all costs.

Bittersweet

Even though I had many lows last year, I also had some great highs. Remember the Coutts apprenticeship I didn't get, and I said I would be back? Well, I meant it. Leadership Through Sport and Business made that possible and I'm so grateful for them. I started my new job at the end of the year, and I felt so ready for my new role but deep down I wasn't, I had a lot of I needed to deal with, but I just wasn't ready to admit it to myself. So, I didn't. I faked it until I couldn't any longer, I literally was at breaking point and one month into my work I had to take some time off for myself. I was so ashamed when I didn't need to be, I just needed to be real. True to myself and true to others around me but it was hard admitting I wasn't okay and that I haven't been for a long time. Imagine being a closed book all your life and the day came where you literally had no choice but to be open, well that was me. I realised I have a lot to work on. My mental health has always been something I struggled with but because I have always been so caught up in everyone else's affairs, being there for everyone else made me neglect myself. Which I felt was fine because as I said I'm not the most loving person even when it comes to myself. My way of coping with stress was to ignore it. As long as I kept busy with a tunnel vision on my career, I would tell myself nothing else mattered. Until I couldn't focus anymore, my mental health was taking a toll on my physical health and that's when I knew I had to take a break and really address my issues as being in denial and keeping up a front is no longer working. Now this definitely doesn't happen overnight I'm still in the process of getting the help I need, helping myself so I don't have a happy ending to my story yet, but I can now say that I know one is waiting for me.

I really had more to say but if I continued, I would be writing forever. I have learned a lot about myself in such a short space of time but I'm still learning. I've learned that it's not good to keep things bottled up, everyone goes through something, but you can't let it break you. I'm dealing with my trust issues, and I've learned to trust my support system, talk to my friends and family about what I'm feeling like. Sometimes you have to be vulnerable in order for people to be able to help you, in order to help yourself. If you're in a dark place you must let people know. Take risks and believe you will prosper. Whenever you feel like giving up, look at how far you have come and remember why you started. I stopped letting my sickle cell define me and I started living beyond my fears. I've faced way too many trials and tribulations for me to stop now. My story is not over, and it will never be, even when I feel like it is, I know I have so much more to live for, so many things I want to say and do to help others. Even when you feel like there's no light at the end of the tunnel keep going and you'll be surprised. Don't allow other people's opinions or the voice in your head to rule your life or make you question your view of yourself. Be authentic, be kind to yourself and others, you never know what someone may be going through so just be gentle. Yes, this thing called life is hard but who said it was easy?

Faustina Edward

I have learned so much from sharing my story. I want to continue being a source of inspiration for others and reach as many people as possible. I have realised that being a positive influence and spreading 'glitter' was not something that I started doing in recent years but much earlier on in my life.

Leave Some Glitter Wherever You Go

I'm not sure what ten-year-old me envisioned her life would look like. Nonetheless, I remain grateful for all the good, the bad and all the things beyond my wildest dreams that have happened to me. I'm also not sure when I decided that I was worthy of changing the world (yes, the world) but it has been the best decision I've made in my life – at least in my 24 years on this earth.

Because of my extroverted nature, people usually think that I've always been this way. However, I was an extremely shy child and barely spoke up. You see, my shyness was not completely because I was afraid to speak up, but it was because of my stammer. Even as a child I was so conscious of my stammer that the probability of being laughed at was enough to keep me muted. Thankfully, my family and teachers encouraged me to get involved in activities even though I was scared. Looking at it now, I think that's when I decided to be my very best so even when my words failed me, my presence, laughter and work ethic would remain with whomever I was around – think of it as glitter.

What would be your honest reactions if a 24-year-old said to you that they really loved glitter? Well, I always seem to include that fact into any conversation that I have. I see the micro-expressions on people's faces, smile then explain why I love glitter and unicorns.

Picture your childhood self, working with glitter on a card for your mum or nanny. Even after you're done with the card, and the teacher makes you clear your station, you are covered with glitter. You go to wash the glitter off with soap and try your hardest to get it off your skin. Of course, you think you've won the battle against the glitter – but did you really? Hours later when you get home, your adult asks whether you worked with glitter at school because there's still glitter somewhere on your body.

I'm almost certain that this scenario has happened to many people at one point or the other. Glitter in my world isn't only the non-recyclable specs that glisten in light. To me, it is positivity and encouragement – something everyone needs. And like glitter, they stick! I wholeheartedly believe you should exude positivity so much that when you leave and after a few days or even years, someone remembers something you told them that positively changed their lives.

When I unconsciously made the decision to change the world in my earlier years, it has manifested ever since. Some may think that you need grand gestures in order to be impactful, not appreciating the value of deep impact. From impacting the class, you serve as a prefect, the students you tutor or the blog you created after procrastinating for years.

During secondary school, college and even university, I was the student who was involved in everything. Having people around me who supported my willingness to take part in various things undoubtedly made me a more confident person.

Secondary school was an almost frightening experience, again, because of my stammer. I went to an all-girls catholic school and pronunciation and diction were a big deal. Reading aloud in class or at assembly terrified me. I remember asking to go to the toilet when it was almost my time to read in class and finding the shortest part of my class's assembly to recite in front of over six hundred girls. Apart from those scary times, I loved secondary school. I was a good student and did my best in assignments and assessments. I took all my responsibilities seriously to be, as Cal Newport put it, "so good they can't ignore you".

During my first year of college, I wanted to revamp the after school programme in my community to help solve the problem of students not being able to afford private lessons despite needing it. On that journey, I discovered that I was passionate about students' access to resources that would allow them to succeed academically. I had the pleasure of seeing them improve not only academically, but through our conversations and encouragement, many of them grew holistically. Truthfully, they impacted my life in such an enormous way that after moving to the UK, I continued to tutor students from disadvantaged backgrounds. To this day, the influence of some of my past students fuels my passion to assist students with their academic journeys.

I founded The Unicorn Project about two and a half years ago with the vision of encouraging people across the world with my content. During the peak of the first UK lockdown in 2020, I decided that I would expand my blog to include a video series called 'Glitter Talks'. The series is based on challenges I've overcome, productivity and of course glitter (positivity). For my first episode, I spoke publicly about my stammer and how I overcame my fear of public speaking. The reaction to that video blew me away. Many people commented and messaged that they would have never guessed that I had a speech impediment because of my confidence when speaking. One person 'slid into my DMs' to tell me how much she was inspired by the video; not only because I had the courage to speak about it, but because I never allowed it to stop me from using my voice. This was extremely humbling because this is exactly what I wanted to accomplish. By encouraging someone with my story, they may feel confident to share their story and inspire someone.

Earlier, I mentioned that I made the decision to change the world. I know, this unknown person from a small island, changing the world? Well guess what – you don't actually have to change the world to change the world. The mission of my blog is to spread glitter and encourage others to do the same. This is where 'the world' comes into play. If you inspire and share some positivity with one person and they do the same to someone else, you have already touched two lives. Now imagine if this chain continues indefinitely!

There is almost an unknown power in being a beam of light. While people say it a lot in speeches and books, if you really think about it, you can quite literally change the world one smile, one encouraging word and one moment of positivity.

Wherever you go, whoever you come into contact with, however you choose to use your voice, remember that you have the power to positively impact someone and bring a smile to their face. After all, it is extremely important to leave some glitter wherever you go.

Mohammed Essakini

Sharing my story has made me stronger within myself, sharing personal experiences with a public that you do not know, is an honourable gesture and makes me part of this global community. I hope those reading, understand that it is within us as individuals to decide the fate of our future in any given situation we find ourselves in, and how we can develop and move forward.

The unknown, the new and diverse touch is the next step towards what matters

As a child of immigrants, there's a constant duality in our miscellaneous existence; the feeling of not belonging fully to a specific culture. Living in a multi-cultural foreign country is where you advance new observations by learning to balance them and of not giving in to any thoughts that believe one is a better culture than the other. Instead, simply embrace, learn and accept constructive diversity.

Looking back, I was a confident guy, always with energy, while observing the perimeters around me and trying to blend in. Having the curiosity of a kid always brought me to a new experience with all I could know; I looked always up to the sky and dreamt of flying. To be in the outside universe was always fascinating. Football however, gave me the reason to always push hard and challenge myself with others.

I was born in Casablanca, Morocco and I was raised at Frosinone, a town near Rome, in Italy. Blending in when living in a country where you were not born is a skill, and now at 23, I can understand what my parents had to go through at the beginning. The high school system in the UK is way different to Italy's where everyone does the same ten subjects and you are seated on the same chair for the whole year. We do get a break mid-morning around 10 am, where we usually socialise for 15 minutes and then finish school at 1 pm.

I was a guy that would rather play football instead of revising or finishing my homework but I was also the same person that would get the job done at the end of the year to pass the subjects. I presume all parents want their child to be smart; my parents pressed me when they had the chance.

The curiosity and visual learning in me, developed critical thinking skills and I enjoyed school more when I started college at the age of 14. After a long talk with my uncle, who I always looked up to, I chose to specialise in IT, even though at that time I had the desire to become a lawyer. I enjoyed programming and I am still enjoying it fully.

Luckily, I never had issues with bullying in high school or college, mainly, because I grew up on the streets where we all knew each other. As ten-year-olds we used to have football tournaments and I was known to be very good at football. It shouldn't be but I have been discriminated against since I was little, sometimes just as a joke. "I'd bleach you like Michael Jackson" or "Go back to your country". Well, I wouldn't take it personally as I always had a sense it was the other person's problem that they couldn't deal with diversity, because more often an other's pride and ego are shown within groups. After all, with some individuals, I was asked more about differences in a constructive conversation rather than them being judgemental. It was strange at times. There would be a lot of laughs, however, you understand the ignorance spectrum.

At the age of 17, I had already moved twice; the second time towards Rome. I guess now the issues I started to realise were whether to get attached to people or places. Well, I found a good group of friends from my class; the college system looked a bit more like the British system. I also started playing with a football team in a youth national league during the summer. However, I did finish the season with my old team and I would travel back at the weekend, take the underground and the coach to Frosinone because it was a chance to be with my childhood mates once a week.

I was only 17 years old and my parents decided to move again, this time to the UK. I couldn't even finish my Diploma in college. It was sad at the beginning but also an exciting feeling because the place was completely different from what I was used to. My parents couldn't speak good English and I felt really bad about this because previously in school, where English was taught as a second language, I had thought that I had no reason to study it. Funnily enough, I found myself in the UK soon after.

I couldn't afford a smart phone so I used to bring my little dictionary to learn some more words and at the same time I would use it to communicate. Imagine how much fun that would be with the help of hands gestures. I then registered in the library where I rented a CD and I started learning the pronunciations and basic English.

I didn't know how the education system worked in the UK. I arrived at the beginning of 2015 and I wasn't sure whether to continue with my Diploma, as my Italian certificate was not accepted. However, I was able to secure a place in Central Beds College for September 2015 but with the condition to start the Diploma from scratch. This was heart-breaking to think of losing those years of study but at the same time I could use the time to improve my communication skills and blend within the system.

While waiting for September 2015 I started looking for a job. I kept watching movies and mainly tuned into BBC news, since they had subtitles and the language was easily understandable for a fresh guy like me. I also managed to save some money from a waiter job to go back to Italy and enjoy the summer with my friends. I took the flight alone this time and it was special since I was able to fulfil my needs in going back to Italy for summer.

For my 18th birthday, I was given a smartphone which I then started using to translate as much as possible. When college started in September I was quite ready. Even though the first year wasn't that great, I attended class but I struggled to understand and write the assignments as they wanted. Also the social life and friendship in college felt cold compared to what I was used to in Italy.

At the end of the year, I managed to pass but with regrets, since I was sure I could do much better. Over the next two years I learned the structures and I was able to deliver all the assignments, gaining the maximum grade, or almost the maximum. For programming, I was the only person in the class to get a distinction in my project. The teacher congratulated me as he never gave a distinction in that programming assignment during all his years of teaching.

The next year I ended up learning by myself and attending class only to keep the attendance or to go through the assignments. I finished college being awarded maths GCSE and D* D* D in my BTEC Extended Diploma which I then used to apply for Degree Apprenticeships, as I thought myself to be too old at the age of 21 to end up at uni. Luckily, I was able to attend many interviews. When I was at the interview, I felt I had the position but sadly this was never the case and the replies were always the same. I thought that it was due to my communication skills, so that year instead of trying for uni, I started working full-time in Luton airport as a sales advisor.

The year after, at the age of 22, I started working for a well-known corporation called Luxottica in St Albans where I also rented a room. I worked as a customer service representative for multiple eye-wear brands, chatting on the phone and via email. People expected high customer service so I used the opportunity to polish my English and Italian as I worked for both countries. In the same year, I passed my driving licence in the UK, then I decided to apply for the computer science undergraduate course at the University of Hertfordshire, near my workplace. I received an unconditional offer. At this point, I ticked all the boxes I set myself five years ago, which were to learn the foreign language as if it was my own, get my driving licence, finish my diploma, enter in uni or a degree apprenticeship, and gain work experience while meeting new people.

I started uni in September while working part time; I was excited. I decided not to move near uni because of work. Previously, I used to party with my mates often but I no longer felt that need. Instead, I had the call to prepare myself for tomorrow so that from the next day on, I could live happy, without worries thinking how in the past I was strong and mindful. I came to this conclusion because I studied the biography of individuals who had made a difference in the world. Those such as

Tesla, Einstein, Cesare, Leonardo Da Vinci, Steve Jobs, Alan Turing any many more. I could see how they had worked and achieved their results, so I applied their experience to my programming studies at uni and in the first year I gained high results.

So far in that I accepted people, time and opportunities come and go, the most important thing is to have faith in myself and in what I can achieve. Hard times are also present and it's down to how we find solutions, that we are honest to ourself and understand the difference between what we need and what we want. I guess there is a lot more to learn but our ideas improve as long as we do not presume that everything is static. Find people that value you or people you can learn from, as everyone has a story and each story could have been anyone.

Bethany Fraser

Sharing my story has made me realise how much I have changed since moving back to the UK, and how the challenges I have faced along the way have helped shape me as an individual. I hope that by sharing my struggles, I can help others realise that they are not alone during their journey to securing their dream career. And that they should never let a setback hold them back, but instead use it as a learning experience.

The Journey Begins with You

As so many people experience themselves, to get to where I am today has not been an easy journey. I have had to adapt to living in a new country, learn to deal with many setbacks and now break forth from university into a career path during a global pandemic. On top of that, I have had to overcome a lack of confidence and sense of not belonging. However, to be honest, if I could go back in time, I would not change a thing as these challenges have made me who I am today. So here is my story so far, and even though I am still learning and growing, here is what I have learned through the challenges I have faced along the way.

As a baby, my family moved to Spain where I grew up attending the Spanish education system and learning the Spanish way of life. For me, it was always an adventure in Spain. I had lots of friends and was known to be a top achiever in class. However, in class I was always the shy little English girl in the corner.

In 2015 my family and I moved back to the United Kingdom. This was an exciting time as it was a new chance to start afresh and get to experience a new way of life. What I didn't realise was just how challenging life was going to get. I was placed in the deep end of a new and very different education system and GCSEs. At the time I had no idea what GCSEs were. I had to adapt to the English school system quickly to match with all the other students as I had come from a different academic system in Spain. It was a big step back for me and my confidence and despite my new resolution to no longer be the shy English girl in the corner, I merely became the shy girl who barely talked in class.

I struggled with talking in group situations and *dreaded* the thought of saying the wrong thing, especially in class. I also felt like I did not belong and was out of place with my new friends, as I just could not relate to anything they did or said. My lack of confidence meant I was quick to doubt myself and my abilities out of fear of being judged.

Through hard work, my GCSEs were successful. However, my A levels not so much. For two years I worked tirelessly putting in a lot of extra work at sixth form and my confidence grew. My predicted grades were amazing but when the exam season arrived, the stress and pressure to achieve the best grades took over. On reflection, having to complete six of my A levels in two days impacted me and left me mentally drained resulting in my grades making me feel like a failure.

Yes, my grades were all a pass, but they were way below what I required for my university of choice and indeed, to study law. I can remember feeling like my dreams were shattered. I had become so tunnel-visioned that I made it difficult for myself to realise the alternative pathways. Luckily, I had been made an unconditional offer to study law at another university thanks to my hard work and my predicted grades. However, I started to doubt whether I truly could achieve a career in law.

Picking myself up and being positive, I commenced at university which again was hard but definitely worth it. Having moved away from home, I found myself living in a studio apartment (this is why you do not leave accommodation to the last minute!). I was in a new location and had no friends at the time. Even when my seminars started, it seemed that all the other students had made friends with their new flatmates and were having fun. I felt alone and isolated making it the complete opposite of what I thought life at university would be.

But through determination, friendships grew, and I finally started to embrace university life. I found the evenings a struggle though, especially coming from a big and loud family household. Even when I did meet up with my friends, I would always have to leave early to make it home before dark as I did not want to walk home alone at night in a city. This led me to not going out, except to university during the daytime. This started to become a big issue. Not only did it make leaving my accommodation harder, but it also impacted my mental health. I did not know who to turn to at times because I did not want to worry my family and did not want to come across as weak to my friends. I was over-thinking every scenario which meant things started to spiral out of control and I felt like I was missing out. Then, one day whilst I was on the phone to my mum, it all just got to me and I let it all out. It was not until I started asking for help that I realised I was not alone. I had a bigger support circle than I thought, from my family members to the friends I made at university.

From that moment, life turned for the better and the following year I chose accommodation with my friends but when I started applying for work experience, I was faced with another challenge. The placements I was interested in wanted top A-level grades, but those that did not want good grades needed previous work experience. I felt like I was being set up to fail, so I did not bother applying. I felt I was just wasting my time with the long application processes.

I then noted my friends were attending career events and that was helping them gain work experiences. I felt that I too needed to follow, or I was going to be left behind, so I jumped in but signed up for way too much. Therefore, I took a step back and realised I was getting nowhere just following the crowd. No company wants a robot for an employee, they want someone who will stand out from the crowd. With that mindset, I started doing things that would help me and took on roles of responsibility within my university. No, it was not the work experience at a law firm that I wanted, but once I opened myself up to other areas I was getting somewhere. This change of mindset led to me being noticed and gained me a place as a Next Gen consultant at TG Consulting.

I started changing the way I think about situations. I now force myself to apply for opportunities because, as I now tell myself, 'you'll never know unless you apply'. This has opened up multiple doors for me, and I even took on roles that pushed me out my comfort zone such as appearing on a podcast. Even though I was super nervous that I would mess up or stutter with my words, I still did it. It is always that feeling of accomplishment that drives me to want to do more. To push myself to be the best version of myself. So, focusing on the positive outcomes instead of the 'what ifs?' makes it all the more worth it in the end and helps keep you motivated.

Leading up to my university years, it is evident that I allowed my past experiences to affect my confidence and hold me back from opportunities. I doubted my abilities and became my own critic. The pressure and stress one must go through these days to gain a degree at university increases each year. The expectations companies have towards their recruits is rising, and the world has become increasingly competitive. However, my advice, gained from my quest so far, is that at the end of the day, no matter what the people around you are saying, we are all in the same boat. Some might have more life experiences than you, but they too were once in your position, so we all must keep pushing on and not be afraid to ask for help along the way. And who knows, asking for help may open up some hidden opportunities that you did not know existed.

In the end, my challenges in life have led me to where I am now, have made me a stronger person mentally and have made me contemplate 'what do I want in life?' instead of following the crowd. Sometimes life is not meant to be perfect, but that is okay because in the end, it means we become stronger as individuals. Life's troubles can help us reach our career goals, making us more appreciative of our accomplishments and more deserved of what we make ourselves.

Alexandra Garton

Writing this piece was a great chance to reflect on how far I have come and all I have to be thankful for. Where I am now is just the next step in my journey; nothing is over or decided yet! I hope that my story encourages someone who feels that they cannot get up off the ground, to open up and ask for help, wherever they can find it. Something good is out there for everyone.

A Series of Moments

How long is a 'moment'? Ten seconds? Two minutes? More? Less? However long you define it as, we're given limited moments in a lifetime, and as they string together, a journey starts to form.

When I think back about my mental health decline, the earliest moment that comes to mind is a few minutes of existential crisis I felt on the first day back at school, aged fourteen. I'd always been a generally happy person, but in this one short 'moment', it hit me like a tonne of bricks: what is the point of living? I didn't have the answer.

I often felt dejected and miserable after that. I think it was a slow decline, but I'm not sure. I recognise it now as the first sign of a looming deeper depression. The summer after completing my GCSEs was long and drawn out – I didn't have much going on and didn't get to see my friends very often. When I did, I felt that they were disinterested in me. I can hardly remember that summer (to say it was so long), and in my mind it has become one very long, lonely 'moment' on my journey.

By sixth form, the symptoms of depression were settling in, without my realisation. I felt low almost all the time, I rarely had any desire or motivation to do anything, and I couldn't imagine what my future looked like – which was difficult, as everyone was very excited for university.

My friends' apparent disinterest in me grew, and I felt incredibly alone. I had signed up early on for three extra-curricular opportunities, but it didn't take long for my excitement and motivation to fizzle into nothing. I clearly remember three distinct 'moments'; all avoiding eye contact with my head of year, explaining that I'd be dropping out of each activity, while he tried to dissuade me.

One place I found solace was at work. I worked at a family theme park, operating rides (and it absolutely was as brilliant as it sounds). There, I felt important. I had purpose, real responsibilities, and a duty of care to our guests. I was putting smiles on peoples' faces with a great team of colleagues, doing something so unique and fun that it *almost* pushed everything else aside. One 'moment' I cannot forget was watching the fireworks display from my booth the day before Halloween in 2016; I stood mesmerised for the whole show, thinking, *"I never want to forget this moment."*

Eventually the time came when I couldn't cope with being around my friends, feeling isolated and rejected. One day, I made a snap decision to take up my classmate on his offer to spend lunch with his friends. To this day I'm grateful for that split-second 'moment'. They made me a part of their lives immediately and have stood by me since. I cannot emphasise enough how much I treasure his and their company, now and while I was at my lowest.

Unsurprisingly, my depression got worse when I started university, and I finally started to think, *"this isn't right"*. Depression sadness is so different from regular sadness; deeper and more desperate, and I felt like I couldn't escape. I had a handful of friends, but I was still dealing with the rejection I felt from my old friends. Deciding to tell them how they made me feel was a deeply sad 'moment' for me, as they weren't interested − but in hindsight, it offered me some closure.

Two months into my second year, I started suffering chest pains and aching in my left arm. Eventually this got frightening, so I phoned 111 for advice. By far the scariest 'moment' in my story is the operator advising me that she was sending a paramedic − I've since learned that most chest pain calls are the second highest priority for an ambulance. I remember very little of the night; I was whizzed to hospital to have some tests, and wheeled about the place in a very uncomfortable wheelchair and my

Winnie the Pooh pyjamas. They diagnosed me with a non-threatening chest condition, but in my delirium, I remembered just one thing I was told: I was suffering from anxiety, and I should make a doctor's appointment.

That appointment was very tearful. I'd already spoken to the student support team, but they were overwhelmed with drop-ins, so the advice they gave me was unhelpful. Thankfully, the university health centre offered mental health consultations, which were longer than regular appointments and generally expected to be quite emotional. I struggled to articulate why I was feeling so down, but the GP sat patiently and talked with me, diagnosed depression, and referred me to a local NHS mental health trust. Like the student support centre, they were absolutely overrun – but did offer me group cognitive behavioural therapy (CBT). That's the big 'moment' I remember in this case; opening the letter which promised help for the first time.

The therapy wasn't the *most* helpful thing, but it could have been worse – a lot of it had been covered in A-level psychology, and the rest focused on healthy habits. I had underestimated the value of this, though; getting into and out of bed at specific times, eating my three meals a day, and making sure I showered and exercised daily didn't fix whatever was broken, but it did give me some stability and routine.

Eventually, though, these healthy habits morphed into less healthy obsessions. I couldn't do anything unless everything around me was spotless, couldn't sit comfortably if my hair was even slightly greasy, and my sleep routine was so clockwork that as little as an hour under or over my regular pattern gave me a migraine. The defining 'moment' here happened at home; something in me snapped, and I screamed at my brother over a minor comment he had made about the way I was. It was a real wake-up call to the fact that I was too fixated and reliant on my habits designed to shut depression out, and that while they masked it, they didn't take it away.

Once I was back at university for my final year, I was filled with resolve and determined to make a change. I moved into a nicer flat, where my neighbour was also a final-year student on my course. I dug out paperwork for extra-curricular awards I'd signed up for but was never motivated to work on. I started working open days for prospective new students, which I thoroughly enjoyed, and met lots of new friends through this. I also made more of an effort to go out and see the friends I already had – their incredible support was heart-warming, and made me feel much less alone. These efforts seem small from the outside, but for me the energy and willpower they took was enormous. My aim was to keep my mind occupied so that depression wasn't such a heavy weight – I wasn't expecting to get anything extra from it. But sometimes, just occasionally, life hands you a bonus.

During my second open day, an academic in my department approached me for a chat. He asked the question I most dreaded; "what are you planning on doing after you graduate?" For me, this was a very loaded question; I had only just started to think that my todays and tomorrows weren't so bad. I didn't know what the future held – I didn't even know what I was going to write my dissertation about, and that was a much more imminent problem. I can't remember what I said to him. Whatever it was, it inspired him to introduce me to one of his PhD candidates. That was such an important 'moment' on my journey – the research that he was doing made me realise that it was my favourite area of my course – why wasn't I pursuing it? Everything is a blur after that; my dissertation topic was decided, I collaborated with them on one of their studies – which led to a published paper with my name on it – and now I'm studying the master's degree I once swore I would never even consider. I've never once looked back.

Life is a series of moments. All of them, even the bad ones, are building to something, even if it's not clear yet what that is. Some moments teach us that anything can happen at any time, or that help is available in places you might not think to look. Some teach us that even the darkest times can have bright moments, or that we're never as alone as we think we are; help is out there. For me, the most important lesson I learned in a moment is to take every opportunity – it could lead to anything.

There are still days where I wrestle with depression, but my series of moments has taught me the most valuable lesson.
Life *does* get better.

Jacob Grimwade

I feel sharing my story has been a great actualisation as to what I have achieved in such a small amount of time and that I can accomplish whatever it is I set my mind to. I hope it has helped others realise that their dreams and goals are not unattainable and that your mindset in given situations is the most important thing to master.

Mind Over Matter

My name is Jacob. I currently live in Colchester, Essex, my hometown. I work a full-time job in the automotive sector whilst running a content creation agency called Euphoric Solutions Ltd. Euphoric Solutions is an agency which specialises in video content, branding and website design for businesses, primarily in the automotive sector. Euphoric Solutions has been a business for nearly two years now. We have created content for businesses and companies including Land Rover and BMW, some achievements we have made within my first five months of graduating from Bath Spa University. Euphoric Solutions is not a single-man operation though. It is run alongside my business partner and friend Brandon, an early school friend of mine. Throughout this chapter, I will tell my story as to how I got here today and what I hope to accomplish in the coming years of not only my business but my personal development.

I am going to start this story explaining my thought process and the way I think. I myself am a heavy believer in positive thinking. I have spent the last 5–6 years of my life trying to master turning negative thoughts and situations in my life into positive ones. Growing up I was 100% negative in my life. During my school time I would not admit this, but I was a heavily low, nervous and scared person. I was afraid of being myself. My early teen years were spent in my bedroom playing my Xbox and struggling with my social skills. I was afraid to try anything and sabotaged my own education, so bad in fact I failed all my GCSEs but three. It was an exceptionally low moment for myself, seeing the disappointment in my mum's eyes as she read my results. My mum is most definitely the hardest worker I know and is a key point of inspiration for myself. Watching the person who believed in me the most read my results was a striking actualisation as to what I could achieve if I tried with my life.

The next three years of my life were the start of who I am today. My three years spent at The Sixth Form College Colchester were where I discovered a lot of my passions including videography, cars and fashion. I invested myself into my education, resitting my GCSEs for my first year whilst my closest friends studied their A levels. I struggled a lot during this time, feeling like a failure or an idiot because I was not studying my A levels with them. When I say I struggled, I mean I was embarrassed to tell people what I was studying at the sixth form. Coming from a past of being socially inept, I struggled to truly be myself knowing I was resitting the exams I should have passed the year before. Come August 2015, opening my results at 7 am and seeing I had passed with a good amount of A grades was an emotionally overwhelming moment for myself. Knowing I had passed those simple exams I had tortured myself mentally about for years, I finally felt relaxed and more confident in my abilities.

My next few years of sixth form I dedicated to finding who I wanted to be. I started my fitness journey, got myself my first few jobs and began picturing who I wanted to be in a few years. My first job was in the kitchen of a McDonalds. Working here made me truly realise how everyone is needed to make the world go round. I never imagined I would work there but for two years of my life, it was where I spent most evenings. I finally left this job after I turned 18 and got myself a job in a Costa for the rest of my sixth form studies.

I achieved some standard A levels and landed myself an unconditional offer for Bath Spa University. University was never one of my plans and was something I applied for on the last day I could submit my UCAS application. I was bored of Colchester and everything it offered. I had spent my entire life there. Full of unhappy memories, I applied for universities which were far away and offered a change of pace. Bath was somewhere I had never visited and when I arrived for my first time, it was the day I moved into my accommodation for my first year of study. I have found that I tend to make more progress when submerging myself in something head first. Moving to Bath to study like this is an example of this.

In Bath was where I was able to truly feel myself. I made new friends who saw me for me which allowed me to actively pursue what I was interested in. I spent my years there pushing my social skills and developing new levels of confidence. I planted the seeds for my prospects, toying with the ideas of starting my own business during my studies. This is when my friend Brandon and myself got back in touch via Instagram. We had been friends at school, editing game-related videos. We were self-taught in video editing from a young age and realised a lot of the promotional videos for local businesses were lacking professionalism. Matching this with our joint interest in cars, we began reaching out to dealerships asking to film their car stock. We struck luck in 2019 when we were signed on to film for a local dealership. Producing in-depth, cinematic videos of car listings was what we began doing. Being given the keys to fun, sporty and fast cars we wish we could own on a regular basis is one of the many benefits of this role. This gave us a steady amount of work to keep our business afloat whilst we searched for more clients.

Starting this business was the true test of my social and business skills. We quickly discovered the best way to sign on new clients was to actively walk into businesses and approach the owners. We found that calls and emails did not truly sell the product we were selling. Whilst our product was good, car dealers could not see the true benefits or trust us from an email. Our social skills in person allowed us to build trust from businesses. We slowly started building up a portfolio of businesses we were working with. Word of mouth is the most effective form of finding work. By delivering exceptional service and becoming friends with our network, we were able to allow our work to speak for itself.

2020 proved the entire world to be a tough year. When the pandemic began, it put the world of business and education on hold. With restrictions in place, I had no clue how I would finish this degree or how my business would flourish. I moved back home to Essex, leaving my Bath life behind. On top of this, I had recently lost one of my closest friends, Graham, to a rare strand of meningitis. This was the lowest moment in my life. It reset how I viewed those around me and made me realise how real it is that anything can be taken from you in an instant. One of my best friends, someone I lived with for just over a year in Bath and spent a lot of my time with, gone. Graham was my first experience with death and is still something I am processing, one year later. I hold him awfully close to my heart and have been using his life as something to remember and use to push myself. I know that he as my friend would be let down if I did not strive to achieve the goals me and him discussed often.

Throughout the pandemic I managed to teach myself an entire module and finish my degree, finishing with a 2:1. This grade felt truly earned and I am proud of myself for attaining it during a difficult and unclear time. With my studies complete, we could focus full time on Euphoric Solutions. Brandon and I, since the summer of 2020, have been able to upgrade our entire editing suite and equipment arsenal. This has opened doors for us, filming unreleased cars from BMW and working with off toad specialists at brands such as Land Rover. Two large businesses we can proudly add to our clientele, providing some of the absolute best content for these companies and their online brands.

Furthermore, with no sight of the pandemic ending, we have continued to push on, securing some large clients and projects for 2021. Clients and projects which could push the business into new sectors and areas we had not imagined. The journey of our business is a journey I am proud to be on, with many more business opportunities revealing themselves as time goes on.

Phillip Gwynn

Sharing my story helped me to not only reflect on how I have gotten to where I am today but to also recognise that facing these challenges are not out of the ordinary. I really hope that my story of finding myself regarding my sexuality helps others who may be currently facing a similar situation because we all deserve to be loved irrespective of gender, sexuality, class and race.

Accepting My Sexuality

Through primary education, the term 'LGBTQ+' was not something I had heard of or come across before until secondary education began. LGBT education was non-existent through this time so I had barely an understanding of the different sexualities and genders out there; if anything, I felt quite lost within it all. Secondary school was secretly a challenging period for me where I possessed a range of thoughts regarding my own sexuality. Since year 7, I was teased for my camp persona and called gay on many occasions whilst a couple of students betted amongst themselves on my own sexuality; as you can imagine, it was not the nicest experience.

Being brought up in an area of Yorkshire where homophobia has always been prevalent in the local towns, I have always found it difficult to come to terms with myself and discover the true me. I would say it was after two school relationships with females that I was more certain that I identified as gay. That is not to say that they were not nice people; they were lovely people but my instinct was telling me something different. However, I never told a soul for the duration of secondary school so the 'love-life sessions' that were put on as part of our education felt incredibly awkward. They were only taught to us in a heterosexual context whilst disregarding every other sexuality in the room. To be honest, I felt quite left out during these sessions because deep down, I could not relate to it at all. There was no support either so it was not like I could speak to someone about my concerns.

I was too afraid to speak to my family about being gay in the past due to their traditional views so for years, I carried this all in my head. Sixth form, which was within the secondary school, was the time where I started to come to the conclusion that I am gay. People have asked me the dreaded question many times: "When did you know you were gay?" It is a question that cannot really be answered with certainty and there should not be an expectation to know either. Having said that, I did feel that sixth form was when I had a good idea of my sexuality. It was just the school environment that held me back from accepting who I really was because of the absence of LGBT education and support on this.

As I embarked on the next chapter in my life (university), things started to look up. The inclusivity was felt so strongly that I started to feel more comfortable with myself. However, I was faced with new challenges, one of which was feeling homesick in my first year. I was so attached to home that I hated living away from it but after a week of settling in with an amazing set of flatmates, the homesickness soon passed. It's completely normal to feel homesick when moving away from home and the university offered an abundance of support on this matter as well as many more.

I have always enjoyed studying geography since school so it was a no brainer to continue this into a degree. Originally, I had planned to study drama and theatre at university but after long thought and consideration, geography seemed to suit my personal choices better. There are aspects of geography you typically expect to study including environmental hazards and global environmental issues but there are some topics which may not immediately strike you as geography... gender and sexuality. It came as a surprise to me at first to be having a lecture on gender and sexuality in my first year but I thoroughly enjoyed the material. This triggered my many years of suppressed thought on the matter and eventually, I decided that it was the right time to 'come out' to my close friends.

'Coming out' is a term referred to quite frequently, particularly in the media (e.g. Phillip Schofield) but the question nowadays is, should this still be an expectation of society? I certainly felt as though I had to do it as part of society norms but personally, this should be phased out as an expectation. A heterosexual has no need to reveal their sexuality so many people like myself will say why should a gay individual have to reveal their sexuality? The media broadcasted Phillip Schofield's news everywhere, describing him as "bravely coming out". The fact is that it should not have to be a brave act because it sends out the wrong message to other people belonging to the LGBT community. It is like the media are referring to being gay, lesbian or bisexual as a brave act in our society; the simple fact is that you do not need to be afraid of who you are.

Unfortunately, we are still in a society where coming out appears to be an expectation so as I seemingly followed society norms, I finally told some of my close friends back home and at university; they were over the moon and could not be happier for me. I realised that after all these years, there was nothing to worry about and I could be who I was born to be. In a way, university felt like a great environment to 'come out' and be free because there appeared to be no judgement. However, I hope no one has to feel like they have to conceal their true self because in reality, it should not concern others but only yourself. It is important to take your own steps and feel comfortable with your own decisions.

I think university teaches you this and I have discovered this myself. University is an exciting time which offers various opportunities and allowing your confidence to grow as a person. My first year involved being a course representative for my peers as well as being a student ambassador, showing prospective students around on open days; duties I never thought I could do in a million years. It is about challenging your own fears that will allow you to progress as a person. Otherwise, if you stay in your comfort zone, how can you ever move forward if you stay within your own bubble? My second year consisted of accepting other duties including my new job in the Students' Union shop on campus and being an employability champion where I liaised between the students and the employability service in order to promote this. One of the best achievements from this has to be helping to lead the planning of an event; leadership is not something I normally feel comfortable with due to my previous lack of confidence. I surprised myself really because I realised that I was not so bad at leading like I used to believe in A-level drama when I rarely used to contribute.

All of these achievements, however, do not come without their challenges. Whilst it appeared on the surface that my confidence was improving, some personal challenges tried to set me back. As I was more comfortable with my sexuality, I found myself in a relationship relatively quickly during my first year at university. It was exciting and new but I have to admit that it did come with complex challenges; I always felt like there was something not right but I could never bring myself to the dreaded conclusion of terminating something that I thought would last forever. Looking back on it, it was the best decision I ever made to focus on myself and put the relationship behind me. You would immediately assume that you would feel lost without that person but actually that is not the case.

Depending on the circumstances, you remember the person that you really are and you stop allowing others to pick away at your character. My advice would certainly be to not allow someone to manipulate you into doing something that they prefer to do. Take control of your own decisions and simply be assertive. It is difficult to do but allowing someone to make you feel bad about yourself or manipulate you is not healthy in any way, shape or form. My final year at university has so far consisted of further opportunities offered to me containing the uptake of the role as a student mentor where I am currently supporting the first-year students who were once in the same position as me. It feels so rewarding to give something back and it is highly recommended if you are considering or currently at university.

My final piece of advice would be to take hold of as many opportunities as possible because this will help dramatically to improve your confidence. Don't feel defeated by the challenges that are presented to you. These knock-backs flourish into something more positive where you can get back up, remembering that you are a great person and are worth so much more than you know, no matter what anyone says about you. If you're someone who is currently struggling with your own sexuality, speak to someone about it rather than holding it all in; suppressing this causes a lot of mental damage. Don't care about what others think of this because making yourself happy is the most important thing. You may think this attitude is selfish but I (and many others) would call it self-care.

As Luke Skywalker says in Star Wars (my favourite franchise), "reach out".

Maariya Hussain

My hope for the future is to witness real equality. I do not want people to feel that they are being looked down upon due to their socio-economic status, race, religion, gender, etc. Sharing my story helped me. It enabled me to open up about things I hadn't previously come to terms with. Writing this chapter made me realise how much I have been through and how strong I am to have overcome these struggles. I am not really a person that opens up to others about my feelings and writing this was a way for me to do this. I hope my story influences others to express themselves and let go of anything that is holding them back

Your dreams are worth every struggle

As a 22-year-old student, I did not think I would experience as many battles as I have had to throughout my academic and personal life. I feel as though I have been looked down upon my entire life because of my socio-economic status and was stereotyped due to the area I lived in. All through secondary school I was humiliated and laughed at for living in an area which was labelled a target for "gang crime" and "drug addicts". However, these struggles, they have shaped me into the person I am today.

Neither of my parents attended university and have worked in low-income careers throughout my education. Despite the fact I was not able to ask my parents for academic support with homework or revising for exams, they were always supportive and encouraged me to do my best. It was difficult for me to watch my friends being tutored for many subjects, but because there were three of us to take care of, it wasn't something my parents could financially commit to. I revised for my GCSE exams using CGP revision guides and attempting past papers I found online. This was a stressful and emotional time for me, as I always wanted to achieve the best grades, but there was only so much I could do by myself. I tried my best to not let it put me down. My parents constantly reassured me that I was a bright student and they would be proud of the results I achieve as I did everything on my own merit. When I received my GCSE results, I was overwhelmed with the grades I attained. Three As and nine Bs, all by myself. These results made me realise that I didn't need money to achieve high grades. I think it's important that other students in the same situation know this and I want to help by sharing my experiences that you can achieve anything if you put your mind to it.

Throughout secondary school, I struggled with both anxiety and racism. It wasn't something I mentioned to anybody and I had to face it alone. I didn't know much about anxiety or mental health at the time. I was a teenager struggling with exam pressure, worried about my grades not being good enough for my future. I felt like I wasn't good enough. Alongside this anxiety and insecurities, I faced racist comments telling me to "go back home" or how Asian people are "taking" all the jobs. I felt like I didn't belong. What hurts me the most, still to this day, is that my grandparents moved to this country to give us a better life. There are so many talented people from various diverse backgrounds whose education and success are undermined by racism. In year seven, I was walking alone to my classroom and I was called a "terrorist" because I wore a hijab (Islamic head covering for women). I remember feeling unsafe and a target. Being a Muslim in this country scared me and as a secondary school pupil, I just wanted to fit in.

Another concern I have is that due to the racist attacks and comments I've seen shared on social media, I worry that filling out the equality monitoring sections when applying for jobs will impact my application. Then I ask myself, why should I be worried? I am not ashamed of who I am. If I am not employable to a certain company, then they are at a loss – not me. My dream is to make my grandparents and parents proud. This motivates me to do well as I want to prove to them that the sacrifices that they have made have been worth it. I also want to prove to myself that I did not need to grow up in a wealthy household or area to be successful in life.

Another struggle I faced was applying for a placement year. Applying for placements and internships can be so draining and rejection emails can be so deflating. However, believe me when I say everything happens for a reason. I received rejection emails stating "other candidates have more experience". I questioned this as the reason I was applying for placements was to gain experience. I wasn't successful in securing a placement and I was disappointed because I needed IT experience. After some time, I finally accepted the situation and was ready to complete my final year of university. A month before my final year was about to start, I received an email from my university advertising a placement scheme. After speaking to my parents about the opportunity, I decided to apply, but I didn't hold any high hopes of getting the role. I am so glad I applied because I got hired! My lack of self-confidence could have caused me to miss out on this opportunity by not believing in myself. Do not let rejection emails put you down as placement schemes can be very competitive. My advice is to keep trying. If you do not secure a placement, try and find experience in other ways by looking for short-term work experiences or voluntary work.

The placement I secured was in learning technology support and it changed my life. My team were amazing. I was never judged for my age or lack of experience, and they gave me lots of opportunities to expand my experience. My role required me to advise and train academic staff on how to use and implement learning technology in their teaching. I was a student training the lecturers at my university! How crazy is that? Throughout my placement, I gained so much confidence. I was being praised for my hard work and I came out of my shell. I was able to train staff on using the virtual learning environment and helped them design exciting and interactive courses for their students. When I saw the positive changes in my life, I wanted to share my experiences with other students to help them make positive changes in their lives too.

I was recommended by my university's Careers team to share my placement experiences in a podcast episode run by TG Consulting. 'The Student Sessions' podcast has helped me develop my character, boost my confidence levels and has raised my career aspirations. I answered questions about my placement and gave advice to the listeners too. I would have never had the confidence to agree to be a part of this podcast if it wasn't for my placement year. I was also invited to be a panellist at a webinar also run by TG Consulting, where I shared my experiences and thoughts on social mobility and being a BAME (Black, Asian and Minority Ethnic) student. I have gained some invaluable experiences throughout my placement year and my work at TG Consulting and I would like to use the knowledge and skills that I have gained to help other students experience a better academic and working life regardless of their background.

This year has been a strange one. We're currently going through the Coronavirus pandemic and it has affected people's lives in different ways. The pandemic hit my family especially hard. My nan passed away after contracting COVID-19 and it has had a massive impact on my life. She was the most loving and caring woman and her prayers kept me motivated to finish university. This was an extremely difficult time, given that we were all in lockdown and I was also grieving on top of a huge change in routine, my anxiety got worse and I struggled to motivate myself to work. Growing up you become wiser, and I knew that I needed to do something about my anxiety as it was affecting my work as well as my personal life. I contacted the mental health team at my university. Taking this step was one of the best decisions I have made. Just speaking to somebody made me realise how many things I needed to let go of. My advice to anybody struggling with anxiety, mental health, racism or bullying is to speak up. Support is available, whether it's through family, friends, schools, colleges, universities or even charities. Just telling one person lifts the worries off your shoulders. I have learned to speak to people I trust and ask for support.

I am currently completing my final year of university and applying for graduate jobs. Although the job market is extremely tough due to the pandemic, I am remaining positive as I know that I will never give up on achieving my dream of making my parents and grandparents proud. My advice to you is to never be ashamed of who you are and don't let anybody tell you that your dreams aren't worth fighting for. Always believe in yourself and your capability in achieving your dreams. If things are not going right for you, don't give up. Your battles make you stronger.

Roberta Johnstone

Writing and reflecting on my story gave me more strength and gratitude for the life I live today as, even though I may have down days where life is intense, or I go through some personal drama, it is nothing compared to the pain and suffering I endured through never understanding my own worth. If I can help someone realise, that no matter how hardcore your inner battle is, that there is a choice to how you feel, then I have done my duty.

I am enough!

Looking at my life today, there is almost no comparison to my past. I am a mummy, a BSc graduate and a MSc student. I am financially independent, emotionally content and mentally sound. Only five years ago I was an isolated drunk, stuck in endless cycles of self-harm, binging, purging and starving. I had a lump on my head the size of a small satsuma from where I had punched myself over and over, fracturing my skull in the process, to try to stop myself from thinking anymore. I was emaciated and living in pain brought on by chronic pancreatitis and other horrendous ailments. I was financially ruined, resorting to shoplifting to get my next drink, and I was mentally destroyed. I was better off dead, but I was too afraid to *do it*. I was only 22 years old.

My ever supportive, and loving, Mum, Dad, Brother and I lived in a Scottish town near Edinburgh where I had a wonderful childhood. I was talented from an academic perspective and, if I do say so myself, I was a bloody good dancer. Everything I did, I strived for perfection.

In the middle of secondary school, I wholeheartedly admit that I became very shallow, very quickly as I strived to become 'little Miss Popular' despite feeling like I didn't fit in. In months, I went from being a fun-loving, joyful, and talented little girl in to an obnoxious, teenage brat but, beneath the ego and arrogance, I was incredibly self-conscious. I was slowly becoming mentally isolated and then, I discovered alcohol.

At age 15 I had my first drink. By 16 I was self-harming, drinking when I got the chance and starving myself, all to try and feel numb. It also shames me to admit that I lost my virginity in a less-than-comfortable scenario through peer-pressure, after which, my 'friends' branded me a 'slag'. From the moment I was labelled a 'slag', I felt so lost and allowed that to become a part of my identity. I thought I could find love by having sex, however my promiscuity put me in a multitude of horrific and dangerous situations, including being raped. Fortunately for me, I had my escape route, I could drink. Alcohol took away my shame and guilt; I finally felt numb which I misconstrued as feeling 'content'.

Just after my 17th birthday I was admitted to my first inpatient unit weighing only 83lbs. The only thing that I learned there was the skills required to become bulimic. Physically, mentally and emotionally I abused my family, isolating myself further and further away from their love however, if you had hooked me up to a lie detector and asked me if I wanted to start again, get healthy and stop my destructive, addictive behaviours, I would have said yes and passed the test. However, I could not stop, and things got worse. Binging, purging and drinking myself into blackout every waking moment became normal.

I would wake up in the morning and consume two pints of strong cider before I had even worked out what day it was. I had been diagnosed with manic depression, anxiety and borderline personality disorder. I went from job to job because I could barely keep a job for more than a month without ruining it through not going in, usually because I had wet the bed again and needed to nip out for more alcohol to mask my shame whilst I dried the sheets with a hairdryer, or I would go in to work so drunk that my bosses would have to call an ambulance to take me home, thus ending that job. I was in and out of hospital constantly through sheer drunkenness and, on one such occasion, I stabbed myself in the wrist with a pen that I stole from a nurse, just so that I could feel something.

Now experiencing alcohol withdrawal seizures if I did not drink in the morning, my Mum tried to intervene with counsellors, psychotherapy, etc., but nothing worked. Despite all of this, I did not think I had a problem with drinking or the other behaviours. I honestly thought they were *solving* my problems. Fast-forwarding a lot of drama, upset and chaos, a miracle occurred. I was offered a place in residential rehab, without which I would be dead in a matter of months and I knew it.

I was sent to a 12-step rehab in Weston-Super-Mare on the 2nd of February 2016. I remained in that treatment centre until the 13th of October in 2017 before I made the decision to settle in a dry house (a temporary home for those who are new in recovery and are not drinking/using drugs) in Bristol. I knew no one in Bristol, other than a few who had also moved previously from rehab I went to and started doing what I was told to do to stay sober: join an Alcoholics Anonymous group, attend meetings, work with a sponsor, do the 12-step programme of AA (if unfamiliar, please do some research) and help others. I did not want to attend AA meetings, but I knew I needed to. The people in these meetings were laughing, joking and genuinely happy, and I wanted what they had.

In a few months I had made a wonderful network of friends in AA and started building a social life. I got into a relationship and even got a job as a mental health support worker! I had even gained enough courage to apply for my Biomedical Science undergraduate degree at UWE in 2017… and I bloody well got in!

Cracks began to show in my relationship. He would have a drink 'every now and then' which, fast-forward another whole year, was a daily habit and he was smoking heroin. My relationship became one of financial, emotional and mental abuse and the daily gaslighting and manipulation turned me in to a shell of my joyful recovery-self. I began isolating again, police and ambulance call-outs to my address became the norm and I had just found out that I was pregnant, and I was terrified. Through a string of coincidences and a hell of a lot of strength, I finally got him out of my life. During and after this time, the connection I had with *real* friends kept me afloat, until I could learn to swim again.

In the middle of my second year of university, I gave birth to my beautiful little girl, Elle. My incredible Mum, who by this point was (and still is) my bestfriend, was there to cut the cord, and one of my closest university friends was there for me to give the necessary moral support through the agony of childbirth. I had made a scrawny, yet gorgeous, little bundle of life and I would do anything to protect her. My abuser continued to cause drama, but I very quickly got a restraining order on him and, consequently, he was sent to prison for several offences against me.

Of course, things have not been smooth sailing in my recovery. I have had my moments in deepest, darkest depression and even went through the terrifying reality of what it is like to live with post-natal depression as my domestic violence relationship came to an end, but now, in my present life, I am genuinely happy. I am driving, having previously drank during all my driving lessons at the age of 17; I obtained a first-class degree in Biomedical Science and I am working towards becoming a Physician Associate through studying my postgraduate degree in the hope that I can help people in their toughest moments; I am financially secure having received two scholarships and a prize for my work in undergraduate; I have incredible friends in my life (KB, SRP, LT, JM; I love you guys) and I am eating disorder, alcohol and drug free since the 2nd of February 2016.

The last thing my counsellor told me before I left for Bristol from rehab was, "You're going to relapse." I look back on that and smile. She said that because she could see a part of me that I did not know existed: I have a fierce determination and a passion for life. It is that determination and the support of my family and true friends that has got me through these (almost) five years of recovery, however tough the challenges. Plus, I have discovered what it really means to be loved. It starts with learning to love yourself. Even if that seems impossible, start by being kind to yourself. Try and do whatever makes you happy and, if you are struggling, be brave and reach out to someone as there is always someone who will listen to you. Whether you relate to some, or all, of my story, I just want to tell you that you are not alone. You are special, unique and you are ENOUGH. Life *is* tough... but it is a gift, I promise you!

Some names have been changed.

Ella Lamptey

I found sharing my story was very difficult. It was never something I had planned on doing, and it was hard to open up. I hope that my story will give some comfort to anyone else who is going through the same journey. I want others to understand that they are not alone and know that everyone struggles. I hope that my journey helps someone to start theirs and, if even one person learns something from me, then I believe that taking part in this opportunity was worth it.

Why do I not feel good enough within myself?

A phrase I have said way too many times and a thought that has crossed everyone's minds at some point. The voice in our head that constantly relays every negative message, every negative feeling about ourselves that we can't get away from. Most people walk around with this voice in the back of their mind, but for me it takes centre stage, every minute of the day. Sometimes the voices disappear, I feel great, I trust my judgements, I value myself and then time's up, the negativity broadcasts louder than before. Each person has their own story and this is mine.

For as long as I can remember, I have internally battled with my self-confidence. Although the irony of it is, if you asked my family or friends to describe me, they would probably reply: Optimistic, Positive, Happy. If you asked me, I would say it's all a big act. I honestly think I deserve an award for Best Female Performance for the years 2013–2020.

I have never truly felt good enough in myself and during my teenage years is where I found myself constantly worrying about what everyone thought of me. I felt very insecure and struggled accepting my appearance. I grew into my body pretty quickly during these years, developing breasts and curvier hips before any of my friends. I must have spent days, upon days, scrutinising every single part of my body. Wondering why I looked the way I did, and why everyone else looked better. I would look in the mirror most days and hate the person who looked back, the face, the hair and the body. Sometimes it was so unbearable, that it was enough to force me into tears.

I knew that I had to do something, I didn't want to feel like this forever. To start feeling positive, I had to learn to love myself both inside and out. Accepting myself was the beginning of addressing my unhappiness, identifying why I behaved in such a negative way towards myself and why I couldn't feel amazing. Needless to say, this process was tougher than I ever thought but I had to remember that nobody is born with a limit on how much self-confidence they can achieve. Gaining back my self-confidence is truly one of my biggest wishes in life. These are some of the ways I am trying to fall back in love with myself everyday.

Have you ever heard of the saying 'you have to learn to love yourself before someone else can'?

It really is true. Self-love allows me to have a more fulfilling journey when it comes to building my self-confidence. Once I learn that my happiness does not rely on anyone else, I will be more inclined to recognise my positivity and it becomes easier for me to reject people or choices that do not match my core values. It is also a key factor in my healing process, to acknowledge the emotions I have and move forward. Release the blame I put on myself from the hurt others have caused me and know how holding a grudge is not good for my journey. I must understand that everyday can bring me different outcomes, whether they are positive or negative, and use the opportunity to grow physically and mentally.

I can not count on both hands how many times I have been told to stop comparing myself to other people and to be honest I never completely understood what it meant until I was learning to feel better about myself. I always thought it helped me learn from others, gave me that inspiration and motivation from falling behind my potential. But what I have learned, although it is a natural form of human behaviour, comparisons are not healthy. They create personal definitions, that allow me to envy areas in my life based on what someone else appears possible. It makes me more competitive to achieve social standards and creates unnecessary stressors and self-esteem issues. I know how hard this mental trap is, and it will take time and great effort to get out of. However, I can't wait until the day I wake up and am happy. Happy because I am myself. I achieved goals because I wanted to. I benefited from personal motivation, reminded myself of my own strengths and weaknesses and counted my blessings everyday. I'm telling you right now, my day will come and I am so excited.

The one person that has been with me from the start of my journey and will be there forever after, is me. I need to start listening to what I want, who I am, and what I can do. I must stop seeking validation from others as it is my approval that matters the most. With my faults and imperfections, I am good enough. I have to renounce all these feelings of not feeling enough and celebrate my outstanding attributes and qualities. I should always remember to never give up on myself, keep trying and giving 100%. Embrace the full effect of my talents, strengths and weaknesses and trust my own process. I can achieve anything and everything I put my mind to.

Although these are the steps I will be taking, my advice to you is to make sure you take every day of your journey at your own pace. Set smaller, more attainable achievements that encourage you to keep going. When it comes to failure, accept it, learn from the mistakes and move forward. On the other hand, make sure you always celebrate your accomplishments and the effort you have undertaken, you deserve it.

My journey is still ongoing, and I will forever continue working on how to feel better within myself. No matter what life brings me, I know everyday I have another chance to work on building my self-confidence. Who knows, I might not ever feel good enough, but I must remember that I am.

I wish you all unconditional self love.

Nia Modley

Sharing my story has been an incredibly reflective experience. I find it easy to forget the things I have been through. It is humbling to remember my past. It has made me incredibly grateful for where I am today, and the strength and resilience I have picked up along the way. I hope my story helps you feel less alone in whatever struggle you are facing right now and know that once you've taken the first step to ask for help, you will be surprised and heartened as to how many people there are who want to be there for you.

Dying to survive

For me it was a coping mechanism. A way to feel in control when I felt so out of control of my life. I didn't wake up one day and decide to have an eating disorder; it was never a conscious choice to restrict, but as soon as I started, I was unable to stop.

I was a gregarious, outgoing, full-of-life little girl, and the world really was my oyster. However, hitting teenage years something shifted and changed within me. I had always been the 'good girl', I was able and for the most part, took life in my stride. However, this changed when I went to secondary school. I felt out of my depth – a small fish in a big pond – and a flood of vulnerabilities came to surface. I felt unsure of who I was, I felt less than adequate, I felt unseen, I felt overwhelmed at the prospect of becoming an 'adult'; I turned to food.

As my diet shrunk, so did my life. My world consisted of little more than school, exercise and my eating disorder. I had few friends and pushed my family away. Anorexia became my best friend. I was going through the motions; showing up when I needed to, but I was so detached and cut off from the world. My anorexia numbed everything: pain, joy, love, you name it I was numb to it. The good and the bad. It successfully convinced me I didn't need anything else. All that mattered to me was that my outward appearance matched how broken I felt inside. I was on the fast track to death and I knew it, but I didn't care.

I hit rock bottom with my anorexia during my GCSE year at school. I was constantly cold; every meal filled me with dread; I fainted a lot and I was obsessed with food. Every waking minute was spent tearing myself apart. I constantly strived to be thinner yet every time I got there it was never enough. I lived in my head and for a long time hid the extent of my struggles. However, this only lasted for so long before it got to a point when my family and medical professionals decided it had gone too far and intervened. I was forced to gain weight, as I neared an extremely dangerous weight for my size. With a lack of coping mechanisms, and restriction not seeming like an option as all eyes were on my weight, I flipped into bulimia.

I had been a highly functioning anorexic. My grades at school were great. I showed up, despite being very sick. However, with my bulimia came huge highs and lows, and I found it so much harder to carry on with life. Getting up in the morning after a night of bingeing and purging often felt too difficult to bear.

I scared myself with the level of intensity of my self-abusive actions. I consider myself a very loving, caring person and would never inflict harm on anyone. But I was certainly capable of inflicting harm on myself. I reflect back to this time as a very painful, lonely period in my life. I had no ability to look towards the future. I was surrounded by people thinking about their next steps, applying to university, and getting excited about life. For me, getting from one day to another felt like a huge ordeal in itself; I couldn't comprehend how I was going to even pass my A levels when I couldn't go a day without bingeing and purging.

Unlike my anorexia, I didn't want my bulimia. Every time I binged and purged, I vowed to myself I would never do it again and yet it would happen the next day without fail. This terrified me. I could no longer convince myself that I was in control of my eating disorder. It well and truly had me firmly in its grip. I remember one day, after days of consecutively bingeing and purging, thinking I absolutely can't do this anymore. I cannot live my life like this. I was sick of my whole life being consumed by the thoughts in my head. I had two choices: recovery or giving up on life all together.

Asking for help was terrifying but it was the best decision I have ever made. I started attending a treatment centre and committed myself to being there for three weeks over my Christmas holidays. I was determined to go back to school, to get on with my A levels and head off to university. However, it quickly became apparent that I would not be returning to school anytime soon. There was no way I could give my all to recovery and get my A levels. This was a devastating reality check. My eating disorder had taken so much away from me. Not only my teenager years, but friends, memories and now my A levels.

I'm so grateful today for that part of me that decided to put recovery first. To drop out of school. To make my mental health my only priority. I effectively had to learn to live again and this was impossible to do while trying to maintain any sort of life I had before.

Things do get better. It may not happen overnight, but it will. Six months of treatment, nine months after dropping out of school, I started at a sixth form college determined to get my A levels. Learning to manage school in recovery was a huge journey for me. My eating disorder was so tied up with perfectionism. I had to learn that my best really was good enough and that there was nothing more important than my recovery.

I got through that year and came out with A-level grades I was really happy with. I still didn't feel ready for university. I was only just beginning to find my feet in life, so I decided to stay at home for another year and work. I managed to do a bit of travelling during this time, venturing off to Australia and New Zealand on my own, something that would never be possible with an eating disorder in tow. I then headed off to university the year after, and the last two and half years at university have arguably been the best years of my life.

Today I have a life I never imagined possible. It isn't particularly extravagant, instead really quite simple. It is full of love. I have real connections with people today. I can curl up in front of a movie with my flatmates and devour chocolate with them without feeling immense amounts of guilt. I feel content in myself, and dare I say, most of the time like myself. I know that my worth does not lie in my body, or my grades, or how many friends I have. I can show up today as a sister, a daughter, a friend. I'm reliable. I used to deny myself the existence of any sort of future, and now I have one. Recovery, from any sort of mental illness, is a continuous process, it's not linear and despite all the good there are still lows. However, through the help of therapy, understanding friends and family, the outdoors, today I have a way to deal with the lows.

I have learnt so much from my battle with anorexia and bulimia. I have learnt about my own personal strength, which is more phenomenal than I ever would have realised. I have learnt that I can't do this on my own. I have learnt the power in asking for help. I have learnt there is no shame in not being OK, that everyone on some level, has their own personal struggles. The reason we don't often know of these is because we are not very good at talking about them. I have learnt that mental illnesses are not a life sentence. Today, in a funny old way, I'm grateful for my eating disorder. It got me through a very difficult period in my life, and it has helped me flourish into the person I am today. I have learnt that life is not easy. That emotions can be incredibly painful, but they won't kill me, that just like everything in life they will pass. I do not need to starve, run, cut or binge and purge them away.

I think I would be doing a disservice to myself to say I'm back to that little girl. I'm a new version of her today, far wiser and braver. I have fallen back in love with the passion she had for life, making the most of every opportunity that comes my way. I am more tender and vulnerable today. I'm not afraid to admit when I'm struggling, because I know I'm only human. I don't try to hide my fears. I continue to show up. Even when life feels impossible. I put one foot in front of the other and before I know it I'm storming ahead. I know that sometimes I may need to take time out and that's ok. Above all, I have learnt my mental health always needs to come first, because as evidenced, without that I have nothing.

Katy Mullett

I hope that in the future I will become a successful businesswoman who has the strength and confidence to not let anything hold me back. By sharing my story, it has helped me to be at peace with my past. I want to help others realise that it is okay to have faced barriers in the past, what matters is accepting them and always believing in yourself. You can do this!

Do not let challenges bring you down, let them rise you up instead

When I look back over the past few years of my life, I realise the pattern of always staying at the back of the crowd and trying to be as unnoticed as I could possibly be. Being classed as the unpopular, ugly, geeky girl in a school where popularity and prettiness ruled the halls, it was very easy for the bullying to begin. I just never thought most of it would be done by some of the people I had trusted for the past seven years of my life. I think everyone can agree that secondary school very simply is one of the main focal points for cruel and spiteful girls to strike their prey.

They say that almost everyone has been bullied at one point or another in their life but only 22% of people speak out about it. It is not easy to speak out if you have been bullied though as some people may feel embarrassed to admit to it and some people may be scared of the repercussions that could come with it. Hopefully, by the time you have read my chapter, you will understand how important it is to speak out to someone. Whether it is: a friend, a teacher, a family member, or even a pet… telling someone, anyone, what is going on will really truly help you.

All through my first year at secondary school, I was the girl that never raised her hand, the girl that never talked in class and the girl that was always picked last; I was the opposite of what everyone at school wanted me to be. Growing up with divorced parents is never easy on anyone and secondary school was definitely not going to be an exception. By having to go between living with my mum and living with my dad throughout the week, it was hard for me to tell them what was truly going on at school. I found myself telling my mum the things that happened at the beginning of the week and my dad the things that happened at the end of the week. Each parent was naturally hearing half the story so neither of them could ever understand all of what was going on. It was so hard not having a parent there the whole time who I could share the whole story with. So, with no parent and no friends to share my problems with, I decided to keep everything to myself because I thought that was the best thing for not only me, but for everyone.

Most people would say that the first year at a new school is the hardest as you have to get used to the routine, surroundings, and the people you are with however, for me, it was the easiest of the five years. No one except for me knew how much I was wanting to change schools but there was no better place to go considering I had already failed at getting into my first choice of school twice before. I was going into the second year of secondary school with less friends, less confidence and more insecurities and doubts.

The second year was almost the same as the first year unfortunately. Although I began to speak more and reach out more, the pain and the bullying increased as well. From an educational point of view, I excelled throughout the year. However, from a social and psychology point of view, I only managed to get through doing the bare minimum. I kept everything that happened bottled up because I did not want to bother anyone with my problems. Little did I know that doing so was going to bite me in the back later on.

So, once again, I was going into the next year of secondary school with less friends, less confidence and more insecurities and doubts, except this time I had a build-up of two years of bullying and unwishful thoughts. The third year was when my year were starting our GCSEs, which did not help as it had its helping share in pressure. Within the first week, I was already struggling and falling behind. It had nothing to do with my academic capability, I just could not focus in class anymore because I was so worried about what people might say to me at break. It took a while for anyone to realise what was going on but that did not bother me as it allowed me to carry on the act at home that nothing was wrong. About halfway through the year I started dating a new guy, but he did not realise what was going on either because by then I had got my grades back up and was better at hiding what was going on. After a school year that felt like it had lasted forever, the bullying had died down a little – do not get me wrong, people still made comments and threw looks, but it was slightly easier to deal with. It was not affecting my grades anymore, just my emotional status.

At this point I was going into the next year with a few more friends, a bit of confidence, less insecurities, and less doubts for a change. It was looking like it was gonna be one of my best years yet – and I was right for the majority of the year. For two thirds of the year, I was sailing through and not letting people's words get the better of me. Towards the end of the year, the first of the big mocks and one of my actual GCSEs were beginning to start. Both fortunately and unfortunately, that was when a teacher first realised that something was going on though, but I guess that is going to be the case when I walked out of one of my exams. I got too overwhelmed with and anxious over the mounting pressure, and during one of my mocks I just got up and walked out; it felt like the walls were closing in on me and I just needed to get out of there. One of my teachers followed me out and I spoke to him for hours about what was going on and it was one of the best things I had ever done. He helped me realise that it was okay to be feeling the way I felt, and it felt like a huge weight had finally been lifted up off of my shoulders. I started feeling better about myself, which helped me reach out to my friends so they could understand too.

So, for the first time in my school life, I was going into the next year with a strong support group of both friends and teachers, and a decent amount of confidence. I had scheduled weekly catch-up chats with the teacher who had helped me the previous year and for the first part of the year, there really was no downside to it. Unfortunately, the people who used to bully me began to find out where I was disappearing to weekly and they started bullying me again because of it. I knew I was incredibly lucky to have someone who I trust to talk to about how I was feeling, but I still had a tough decision to make… would I carry on talking to the teacher and put up with the bullying? Or would I stop talking to the teacher and hope that the bullying would stop? Eventually I decided to continue talking to the teacher and just try to block out the bullying. The rest of the year was tough, but I just kept my head down and got on with it.

By some miracle, I managed to pass all of my GCSEs – some exceedingly well, and some I was lucky to at least pass. There was then the issue of where I should go and what I should do next academically. I had to get away from who and what I knew so I eventually decided to go to a college that was fairly far away from my previous school life. I knew I had to get away from it otherwise it would just hold me down. Sometimes a change is good and sometimes it is bad, but for me it was the best thing I could ever do. Meeting new people and having the possibility to make a fresh first impression really helped my social life. By meeting new people, I found the capability to open up to some of them about how I was feeling, and it has helped me more than anyone could ever know.

From all of this, I have learned that it is better to admit and be honest to yourself about what is going on and how it truly is affecting you. Also, I now know that whenever I am going through a rough patch, I just need to look back over how far I have come and remember that I can do it.

My advice to you would be do not be afraid to make a change but only if it is what you want and will benefit yourself. Also, do not be scared to tell someone how you are feeling because, as long as you trust them, they will be able to help you in one way or another. You never know, they could have been through a similar thing and will either know who you should talk to or know how to help you themselves.

Will Rogers once said, **"Don't let yesterday use up too much of today."** You should try to start each day new and with a smile, and always try your best at everything.

So, remember… be strong, be happy, and be the best you can be – and always, always, ALWAYS believe in yourself. You can do it!

Lydia Oldroyd

I hope my future is full of security and happiness. I wish to work in an environment with colleagues I trust, where there is opportunity to progress career-wise and develop myself. Through writing this piece I was able to reflect on what has been a difficult year and if anyone takes anything away from reading this, I hope you know you are worthy of security and happiness.

Progress is never linear
Looking back, I think what I have struggled with most is accepting that I deserve to be where I am.

I went from a very rowdy, small primary school to a huge high school where suddenly I had to try very hard to make myself stand out. Often at school naughty kids would be praised for behaving for a day, whilst those who achieved consistently would fade into the background.

I was always a high achiever through high school and college. I put myself forward for everything I could and was often asked to represent the school at events. I stayed late after classes to revise for exams and alongside studying, I involved myself in every music group I could find. After seven years, I had been playing in 11 hours of ensembles a week: jazz bands, choirs, classical orchestras, Dixieland jazz groups, you name it. When I wasn't revising, I was playing piano for school open evenings and after only three years of playing saxophone, I was a grade eight distinction player.

At the age of 17, I had achieved a week-long placement at Cambridge University's Trinity College law department. I had the privilege to work with top-class academics on mooting skills, discover brand-new legal concepts while also learning to be adaptable and think on my feet. Not long after, I had work experience at one of the top global law firms and a week of work experience at a leading chambers in Leeds.

On paper, everything was going brilliantly. I was succeeding in my studies, I had excellent work experience and a roster of skills to call on. But then August 2019 rolled around: results day.

I had dreaded this day for a while, some might call it a 'gut feeling'. That day for me consisted of a lot of tears and a feeling that I have retrospectively realised was heartbreak. I had my heart set on studying law with international studies at a Russell Group university but I woke up and found I had been rejected.

As a smart kid at a state school, it was expected that I would go to one of the elite, red-brick institutions; constantly told to break the mould and reach for the best. So to hear I hadn't achieved the grades to get in, I felt I had let not only myself down but everybody who had been a part of my educational journey.

Once at university, I realised I had no cause for worry. I found myself in the classic 'fresher' experience of making fast friends and having too much fun. I managed to keep up with the workload and pushed myself to try new things – a badminton society, for one. However, I soon found myself distracted. Making the jump from living and working at home, straight to living in a house with 11 of your new best friends caused a slip in my grades. New and intimidating professors, qualified to the highest extent, made me nervous to ask for help.

By January 2020, I had scraped through my coursework. On university open days, they tell us that A-level Law is not required as it can skew your first-year university perspective, and I found myself victim to this. The heartbreak I felt on results day was just as prevalent at this time with my grades dropping and not attending events as I had in college. However, I do think this was what I needed. I was used to trying hard at school, pushing myself, but I never really *needed* to do it. After the first semester, I signed up for every event I could fit into my schedule. I attended practice assessment centres, lectures by brilliant academics, and I was finally ready to focus on what was important: exams.

March 2020 brought about the most unpredictable life change. We were uprooted from our student accommodation and brought right back home. A month later, it felt as though I had regressed back to my 15-year-old self. Living back in my home bedroom, I picked up old hobbies and spent as much time in the summer sun as possible. During the run-up to exams, I found my work ethic and encouraged myself to revise each module to the best of my abilities. My best tool during this period were my friends. After going through a hurtful breakup, I reconnected with my support network – including my brilliant friends from law school that I found myself previously isolated from – and we worked together to get through revision, the exams themselves, and every piece of news that the BBC had to announce.

Never having taken exams online, this was a period of adapting to the new. I took up extra credit classes during the summer to help myself adjust even though I naively thought the pandemic wouldn't affect my second-year experience. Having the French classes to focus on gave me purpose whilst I would have been otherwise listless at home. Following these classes, I met two wonderful women who continue to be a support for me, and I had the opportunity to work on a reflective portfolio of my time developing my language skills.

Having put my heart into my exams, I am so proud that I pulled up my overall grades. Moving into second year in September 2020, I was hugely apprehensive. Living without my parents again, with less than half of the people I had in first year, during a pandemic, was something else I simply had to adapt to. With university changing our timetables so that we only did one module per six weeks, I found myself with a lot of free time. I spent the first month of the term finding extra classes and events to occupy myself. My portfolio was due and my first university online classes were starting, yet I found time to take up writing classes and a place on a commercial awareness scheme.

I ended 2020 with a first in criminal law. The journey I'd been on through 2020 has fundamentally changed me as a person. Having no option but to be self-reliant and work on who I am has been one of the most eye-opening experiences of my life. Ultimately, I am proud of myself and I am beginning to see that I am worthy of everything I achieve. Moving forward, I am looking into applications for experiences and jobs in the legal sector. Despite having hugely valuable work experience and a depth of knowledge in this sought-after field, I still felt myself unworthy of a career in this job market. My A-level results (along with some first-year experiences) left me with a serious case of imposter syndrome. However, through 2020 I have grown to understand that I should base my success from my efforts. I may not achieve outstanding grades every time but if I am content with my knowledge and the effort that I went to procure it, then I should be proud of myself.

I am working on developing my skill set further. My degree is hugely important to me, but I wish to keep up my extra-curricular pursuits alongside studying. I am continuing my French language studies, have booked taster events in Mandarin and Russian, and I am searching for a jazz band to join. With the ground-breaking release of the COVID-19 vaccine, it (hopefully!) won't be too long until life returns to a semblance of normality: getting to go back to in-person events, classes, see friends, travel, live life to the fullest. While I can say that I have been beyond lucky in this pandemic to have not experienced any loss or much true hardship, I feel that – for myself – this has been a valuable time of introspection that has benefited me massively. I don't think my imposter syndrome will miraculously disappear but after focusing my efforts in second year and experiencing vacation scheme applications, I do see myself as better equipped.

Going from A levels to first year then second year of university, the change to my character and my drive has been indescribable. Every year I gained more valuable experience, becoming more prepared to tackle life as a law student – and, one day, a lawyer. However, to this day I will never forget my roots in music and the strength they gave me to pursue what I am passionate about.

Amy Roberts

Sharing my story has made me realise just how much I have overcome, and I should believe in myself more. I hope that my future self continues knocking down obstacles. I hope that by sharing my experiences that other disabled students feel empowered and see that disability does not mean inability.

Disability Does Not Have to Mean Inability

Starting university as a mature student in my mid-20s was somewhat tough enough. It was a weird middle ground between being 'too old' for the majority of other students, who were in their late teens, and not having 'enough responsibilities' to fit in with the community of mature students. But I was doing alright – I had made friends and was enjoying my student life. Then, around the start of my second year, my health conditions started to unravel. By my fourth and final year, I had to accept that I had acquired a disability. Now that really threw me! In fact, it pretty much turned my life upside down. On reflection, I don't think there is ever a 'good time' for something like this to happen. I think I'd have felt just as blindsided if this had happened at any other point in my life – while I was in a job, between jobs, or still at school or college.

It all started with just a bit of niggly pain in my hip. Turned out I had a developmental condition and a rare disease which meant I had to have two operations during my studies, one of which was a hip replacement. Little did I know at that point that this would lead to my development of CRPS (Complex Regional Pain Syndrome). CRPS is a chronic pain condition which brings me daily delights such as constant pain, mobility issues, exhaustion and brain fog, amongst other things. I need crutches and a wheelchair to get around now – that took some getting used to! You never seem to see 'learner wheelchair-drivers' do you?! It took a while to accept that I needed them too. I would try to hide my crutches in photos, and worry that people would think I was 'faking it' when I got out of my wheelchair to stretch my legs. Letting go of those unhelpful thoughts has been challenging, but has definitely helped me in my journey towards acceptance of my disability, a journey that I'm still on.

When all this began, I was searching for a placement as part of my Psychology degree. I spent a thoroughly enjoyable placement year within an educational psychology service, and felt very fortunate that they showed such understanding and flexibility in terms of my health conditions. Now fast forward to the final year of my degree. By this point, I had been told that I would always be in pain. Always. For the rest of my life. I was in the early stages of what I now call my 'grieving process', I was grieving the 'old me' while trying to make the most of my 'new normal'. To put this into a bit of context: I can't go hiking anymore and I really miss that, but… I am also really thankful that I was able to complete one of the world's toughest day hikes (Half Dome, USA) before I became disabled. What is it they say? Making the most out of a bad situation? Well, sometimes, that just means looking a little harder for the positives. One of the big positives to have come from my situation is that it has helped me to make fewer assumptions and judgements about other people, particularly those with a disability. I have experienced first-hand how rubbish people's assumptions and judgements can make you feel. "You're so lucky you get more time for coursework and exams" … "Ooh what have you done?" (assuming it's an injury when they see my crutches).

So there I am, facing all the conflicting deadlines of my final year of uni, wondering how on earth I'm going to get through it. I struggled to focus and had real difficulty finding the right words in assignments. I fell asleep in the middle of doing my essential reading. I missed lectures and other sessions due to high pain days and healthcare appointments. I spent days crying about how much I had lost because of my disability. I think it's fair to say that I was feeling pretty low at this point. I knew I needed help, but I didn't know what that help looked like. So I reached out to ask for help – for me, this was from the student support services at university, some of my lecturers and my personal tutor. I was anxious because I didn't know what help I needed and I certainly didn't know what help was available.

It also made me feel kind of like I was giving up my independence. I have always been a very independent person and it took quite some time for me to realise that asking for and accepting help does not mean relinquishing independence. The help and support was there so that I could hold onto my independence and to ensure I could work to the best of my abilities, despite my disability.

So, what help did I get? Well, here are just some of the things that were a massive help to me! I had a note taker in lectures for when I couldn't concentrate or when I missed lectures. I had an ergonomic chair in lectures and at home, so I could still study from home when I was unable to go on campus. I discovered text-to-speech and mind-mapping software, which made a huge difference when my concentration was lagging. I started being more open with my lecturers too – having discussions with them helped me to keep on top of things. I am so glad that I asked for help. I'm not convinced that I would have completed my studies without it.

I had to work a lot harder to produce the same standard of work that I used to. It also took a lot longer (thanks, pain brain!) and involved a lot more breaks! I had to adjust the expectations I put on myself (which was not easy coming from a girls' grammar school where anything below a 'B' grade made you feel like a failure). Before things had gotten difficult, I had been on track for a 2:1 in my degree, perhaps even a first (the highest grade you can get at uni). I was always striving for those top marks in my work. But then CRPS happened, and I had to work on being OK with lower marks and expecting less of myself. Eventually, I told myself that I would be happy just to pass everything, and that anything more than a pass was a bonus. Then results day came along. I was ready for whatever was coming. I knew that I had worked as hard as I could on my assignments and in my exams, and I knew that I had put my all into my dissertation. Next thing I know, there in front of me, in black and white, was the fantastic news that I was now the proud holder of a first-class honours degree in Psychology! I could not believe it! I struggle to find the words at the best of times these days (cheers again, pain brain) but, that day, it felt like the words to describe how ecstatic I was just didn't exist! It finally felt like all that hard work and pushing myself, sometimes to my absolute limits, had been worth it. Finishing my studies was amazing in itself. But finishing my studies *and* achieving such a good mark, in spite of the challenges and barriers I had faced because of my disability, was phenomenal!

Now I want to use my disability for good. I want something positive to come out of my experience of living with a disability. For a long time, all I knew was that I wanted to be in a job where I would be helping people in some capacity. With some guidance from a careers consultant, I came to realise that my passion is to help and support university students with a disability. I had already been doing this during my final year. Suggesting improvements that could be made to support disabled students (things I hadn't noticed until seeing them through the eyes of a disabled student). Writing articles for students about disability and employability. Making suggestions as to what people should consider in terms of language when talking and referring to people with a disability (for example, some individuals prefer person-first language – 'person with a disability' – whereas others may embrace their disability in a different way and so may prefer the term 'disabled person').

Now I have a clear idea of what I want my career path to look like. Let me start here by saying that no two people with a disability are the same. Even with a shared diagnosis, or similar symptoms, the experience of being disabled and how it affects people can be very different. Disability can be a very small or very big part of someone's identity, or perhaps somewhere in between. Regardless, at the heart of it, is a person. An individual. Someone with their own unique dreams, wishes and expectations of how they should be treated. *My* dream is to pursue a career in which I can be an advocate for students with a disability and contribute to improving the support and inclusive facilities available. I want to educate others and raise awareness, and work towards normalising talking about disabilities.

If I could share one piece of advice, it would be this:
Be yourself, disability and all! Think about all the strengths and skills you have developed as a result of, or even despite, having a disability. It probably means you are a creative problem-solver, and that you are super resilient and empathetic. These are all part of what makes you awesome! It does *not* mean that you should be afraid to ask for help. Think of it as 'sharing your disability' rather than 'disclosing' it – it's nothing to be ashamed of! And if help and support can allow you to be the best version of you, then why wouldn't you ask for it?!

OK, so that was more than one thing. Like I said, this is my passion! Now, go be the best you that you can be.

Mamadou Sow

For anyone who is facing similar challenges to me, and wondering if you can do it, my advice is: you have got all you need, just believe in your abilities. I am not close to where I want to be, but I am positive that I will get there.

My bumpy journey in a foreign country

In July 2015 I arrived in the UK from Guinea (Conakry). I still remember how it felt to land in a country where I did not understand a word of what people were saying because English is not a language spoken in Guinea, and neither did I. So, the first thing that came to my mind was how am I going to understand English and then be able to pursue my studies as that was the main reason my father brought me here in the UK. To say that the challenge was huge would be an understatement, but since I spoke French, which is the main language spoken in Guinea beside other dialects, my reading skills in English were much better than my speaking skills, and that gave me some sense of relief and also made hopeful that one day even if I will not sound like 'David Cameron', I will be able to speak English fluently.

Therefore, after a few weeks of my arrival I decided to start learning the language, but when I went to College Green for a pre-enrolment test, I was quite surprised by the result I got – I remember clearly what the lady who handed me the result said – "Mr Sow your writing skills in English are very good" and clearly, I thought she was just being sarcastic, but then I realised she was serious. I still can't explain how much that comment impacted my learning journey, it made me believe that I can learn the language and be able to pursue my higher education studies. And within a year I was ready for an IELTS Test which I passed with a grade that could get me into most universities in the UK as I scored

6.5. So, from that moment I became quite convinced that I can achieve anything I want if I keep trusting my abilities which is quite difficult sometimes, especially being in a foreign country where we often face rejections.

After that I decided to apply for university as due to my previous studies in Guinea, the only qualification I needed to get to university was English. However, applying for university here in the UK was not an easy process for me, because I had no one to turn to in terms of guidance and support as I am the first person in my family to attend university, not only here in the UK but in life in general. So, I struggled a lot to figure out what steps I needed to take in order to make my application successful. When I first started my application on UCAS, I was not sure whether it would work out, but I was determined to get it done anyway. So, I followed the procedures and eventually managed to complete the application on my own. I remember the feeling I had on the day I submitted the application – although I was not sure whether the outcome would be positive – I felt very relieved and hopeful.

A couple of months later I received a notification from UWE Bristol saying that they made me an unconditional offer to study the degree of Politics and International Relations which was my primary choice. I was incredibly delighted to hear that from UWE Bristol. So, I did not delay accepting the offer because Bristol was my first choice and therefore, I thought it was the best offer. And my time at UWE during the last two years has proved to me that I was not wrong because UWE Bristol has not only been supportive, but also the most accepting and empowering educational institution I have ever attended.

So far at UWE Bristol my student journey has been much more than just attending lectures and seminars as a student. The inclusion for all that UWE Bristol aspires has given me an opportunity to be a mentee which resulted an internship that I greatly enjoyed. The internship was with the international team for the Mayor of Bristol. My mentor was the Policy Advisor for the Mayor.

The International Team promote Bristol throughout the world and liaise particularly with twinned cities, such as Hanover and Bordeaux. This resulted in great opportunities to be involved in meetings within and outside the Mayor's office where real issues were being discussed and decisions made. I further enjoyed the opportunity to shadow the Mayor several times – particularly during his meetings with the UNHCR Ambassador and during visits to deprived areas. The team allowed me to contribute as well. I conducted research into events in Bristol and twinned cities to help with the promotional effort.

I discovered things about myself. I can understand how the international relationships work and have an aptitude for the research they needed. I learn well in a business environment and am quick to understand new subjects. I also discovered weaknesses, such as my knowledge of how local government is involved internationally. Another aspect I was unfamiliar with was the difference between academic and corporate styles of written communication. I worked hard to correct these weaknesses.

When I first met with my mentor, I explained my career goals of entering international diplomacy and ultimately run for the presidency of my home country (Guinea). I further explained that I had only started speaking English – as a third language – three years ago. He was impressed by this and my ambitions. Clearly, he had a strong idea of what would help me on this path because the placement has substantially increased my awareness of this dimension of politics, has granted me extraordinary opportunities to witness and to participate in these efforts whilst continuing to improve my language skills. I have gained new contacts as well – people who are happy to support my continued development and will be useful in my career ahead.

The placement really highlighted the value of good leadership. Seeing how the Mayor and the councillors dealt with issues has made me even more certain of my career aims.

Apart from the opportunity to see real work in action, the primary benefit of a mentoring and placement programme is the acquisition of skills that are applied in that real environment, rather than those learned in just an academic environment. Now the placement has ended, I can see how I have gained truly practical real career skills that are rarely considered.

How to act in meetings. How to learn by shadowing. Time management. How resources are applied to a project. These are all transferable skills and will be invaluable in the future. An unusual technical skill I developed during my research was to search for specific sites in both English and French. As my range of languages increases, I am better able to apply them to the work I do.

Now that I am in the final year of my degree, I must admit that it feels quite stressful thinking about what the future will be like after graduation. However, I am trying to do my best to make the most out of my final year although it's not easy with the current situation of this pandemic. I have been trying to get as much involved as I can, both within and beyond my studies. As a result, in last November 2020 I was very delighted to be offered the role of BAME (Black, Asian and Minority Ethnic) Students' Advocate in my department at UWE Bristol. As a BAME Students' Advocate, I have to proactively engage with BAME students and groups to understand their needs and experiences of UWE Bristol and provide a representative voice to allow students to openly share their views. Also, the role requires to develop and maintain contacts with staff including academics and professional services staff.

So, as a BAME student myself, I see this role as a chance to not only bring some changes but also to facilitate the learning journey of my fellow BAME students for years to come. Although navigating this role with my final year studies is quite a huge challenge for me, I am greatly enjoying the experience and for meeting a community of people who have so many interesting views and opinions of which I can relate myself in terms of the challenges we faced and continue to face in the UK.

The final point I would like to share here is that I am delighted to see that all the struggle I faced since my arrival in the UK has inspired my younger brother so much that he decided to follow my path towards achieving his degree in Computer Science at UWE Bristol as well. During his application process, he was fortunate to have an older brother who had been through the process which made it much easier for him. That made me realise that no matter how small a breaking-barrier action might be, it can have a huge positive impact on other people. I have understood that a very small action can open a very heavy door, and so I do have to take actions because I do believe that barriers must disappear.

Reagan Spinks

Sharing my story forced me to relive some troubling childhood memories but also made me realise that these experiences shaped me into the strong person I am today. My experiences have caused me to be sensitive, but I know that I shouldn't beat myself up. Expressing my story on paper has shown me that I still have a lot of work to do and that I'm definitely not alone in this journey. I hope that in reading my story, young and older queer folk may feel reassured in knowing that they are not alone in how they feel or what they have experienced. I hope I can also help allies to have a better understanding of what it is like for some LGBT+ individuals.

The Glass Closet: Learning to accept yourself

I have always been an extremely sensitive person; I often take things to heart and get hurt if I cannot please everyone. This may stem from a speech problem when I was younger. I went to a few speech therapy sessions when I was little and have always had a problem with spelling and sometimes reading. Although never diagnosed with dyslexia, it runs in the family and to this day it gives me some grief. As a young child, I always felt embarrassed when asking for a spelling four times or if I stuttered on a word when speaking. Friends laughed at me or called me stupid and it got under my thin skin.

When I was younger, I felt extraordinary pressure to like certain things: sports, girls, cars, rough-housing. There was also this expectation that I should stay away from other things: dance, singing, the colour pink, princess films. These expectations came from a toxic mixture of peer pressure, the media and my innate desire to please everyone and feel like I fit in. However, I did not fit in, and that is something I tried to fix. I tried football club, played kiss chase with the girls, and even tried to get some of them to be my girlfriend. None of this appealed to me, and I was never any good at it. In year 5 I got my Mum to cross-stitch a bunny onto a card and made my friend write a personalised poem inside. I put the card and a rose into this girl's drawer and by lunch, it was shoved back into my own. Gutted that my courting did not work and determined to still find a Valentine (and fit in) I went to the other class and gave them to a girl with the same name. In choir, I convinced a girl to dump her boyfriend to go out with me instead, right in front of him. During this time, I was growing more into my feminine side, and it showed apparently. I was mocked and bullied for the way I spoke or walked. My thin skin was getting thinner and to get back control I retaliated and was sometimes mean myself. Kids can be awful. By now I had started seeing boys in a new light… I started fancying them. This was awkward as I knew it was not right and, well, I had a girlfriend. I had to hide this feeling, go into hiding. I went hiding in the closet.

Secondary school – first time having to wear a blazer and tie, mixing with new people, and having strict teachers. It was scary but that is why I found so much comfort when I made a new friend. He was the first male friend I would consider to be my best friend. We went to each other's houses, went into town for fish and chips. Life was great. The thing about friends from different schools was they did not know you; it was a clean slate free from the past of bullying and judgement. I could be whoever I wanted to be. I got more female friends and confided in them; I told a few that I was gay. It was exciting, liberating almost, to be myself but not enough where I felt comfortable telling everyone. With new friends also come new bullies. With older children come stronger boys with stronger words. Almost every other day I would be called gay, or worse, and be asked if I like boys. People started seeing the closet. In my class, there was this incredibly smart boy and everyone liked him. I was very jealous and madly in love.

After about a year of an amazing friendship with this boy I liked, I told him over MSN that I fancied him. Four years went past of not talking to each other anymore, four more years of name-calling and questions from everyone, even my best friends. I had to remain in the closet but also wanted to do things I liked. I started dance and musical theatre classes. I appeared in a few shows and attended summer workshops to perform on three different stages in Oxford. The closet was becoming more transparent with each day. I never fell out of love with that boy, but I had many more crushes. During this time, I was still being bullied and had a constant internal battle of wanting to fit in but knowing my sexuality would not let me. I went to a school counsellor and spoke with my Welfare Manager. She asked me what was wrong, and the words would not come out. I wrote on a piece of paper and handed it to her. I felt ashamed and sick. The previous times I came out to friends it was exciting because it was new and secretive. But now everyone saw me in the closet, and I saw people looking back at me through the glass closet. It was time to either pretend I was not gay or to come out. I chose to fight myself and stay in. A choice that made me incredibly miserable and hateful towards myself. I hated the notion of being gay and not feeling normal. I hated the fact I was bullied and that I couldn't flirt with a boy as the lads could with the girls. I hated that I had to 'come out' and why the straight kids did not. Why must I tell people I like boys when I already get bullied for it and it is just taken for granted that you are straight? It did not seem fair.

During my school years I still struggled with my spelling, and doing tests or exams was incredibly difficult. After a month of doing a spelling course at lunch break, I had not improved and was never asked to do the course again; they just left me. To avoid a big commotion, I often cried silently during tests and during my English GCSE exam, I cried through the whole hour.

I enrolled in a college but after my first taster day, it was not for me and I quickly got into my school's sixth form. Sixth form is incredibly hard in terms of studies; I would even say it is more challenging than university. If you ever struggled or are struggling, do not worry, you are not alone, and it does get miles better. Coming to my final exams, I again got into an incredibly sad and stressed mood. I was becoming depressed. I was told by my school nurse and counsellor I had to come out to my parents and best friends if I was to start feeling happy again. That night I wrote a letter to my Mum and got her to read it in front of me. She turned, smiled, and said, "I know." I felt immediately better. However, my journey was not over.

I moved into halls and waved my parents off with a mug of vodka that was put into my hands by my new housemate. We sat down and introduced ourselves. One asked me very straight (excuse the pun). "Are you gay?" With just a moment of hesitation, in front of five random people I had just met, I said, "I am gay." He proceeded to interrogate the next person. That was it. No one said 'good for you' or asked any personal questions. My first year at university was not easy. Moving away from home and becoming an independent adult was hard. I was getting into my sad and stressed mood again. I got fantastic grades and moved into a new house for my second year. As the year progressed, the nights were drawing in and I became depressed again. I felt I was not doing my best and thought my housemates hated me. I had this voice in my head that hated the fact I was gay and how much more difficult it was to interact with people, to fit in with the lads, or to find love. I hated feeling like this and wanted to feel happier. I went to therapy and took medication. It was a challenge and a lot of work, but I managed to keep my head high and made some new friends while learning to let go of others. I moved into a new house with new friends and started to feel happier for longer. I became a student representative for my year, championing my peers' views and issues. I finished my degree during a global pandemic to achieve a top 2:1. Most importantly I was starting to love myself more and slowly but surely throwing away those shards of glass.

This is not a story about how my life is now perfect, far from it. I still struggle immensely with being kind to myself and allowing myself to be sensitive. Some days I often over-think and punish myself, pushing away friends and family. No one has a straight and narrow path to happiness. It has bends, branching paths and fallen trees to climb over. This is what makes it all worthwhile. Always remember that your path, however bumpy or winding it may be, it is not a lonely path. You will meet many on your journey. Some will be your best friends for a mile or a few steps, some you will fall madly in love with, some may fall madly in love with you. But you never have to do it alone. Reach out and take someone's hand and do one more step.

Grace Thompson

I hope that by sharing my story, that I can be a great role model to other young people and hope to one day stand in front of others and share my story. It's important to come out of your comfort zones and sometimes admit to ourselves that we can't make it on our own and it's OK to let others help you.

A barrier is not a limit and you are not a failure

Quite often I ask myself: "Is there is a book or a manual that explains how to deal with emotions, barriers, or simply, how to deal with everyday life?" Very often I can't find the answer, because there probably is no book that can give me the answers that I am looking for.

I was born in Ghana, in Accra, the capital of Ghana. I was living in a compound house with my dad's brothers, their wives and their children. From the little that I can remember from my childhood, I used to have a simple life, after all, I was only a child. I woke up in the morning and got ready for school. I had to make sure that I was clean all the time, as even white socks had to be completely white otherwise there would be an issue at school, meaning, you were going to be beaten with a cane.

At the age of seven, I moved with my mom to Italy, where my dad had been living for about five to six years. The day my mom first told me that we were going to be staying with my dad, I was very happy, but I didn't realise until I got on the plane that I wasn't going to see some of my loved ones for a very long time. However, I was also excited because I missed my dad throughout my childhood and this quite often made me feel very jealous of my cousins who had their dad around, although my uncles tried to play the part of my dad, they weren't him.

When I arrived in Italy, I noticed many things that were different from where I came from. There were people of a different colour to me and who spoke a different language. Not only that, but the buildings also appeared very long and the weather was cold. I saw how the leaves changed during the autumn, as well as seeing snow, rain hail and the change in weather during the spring and summer for the first time. When I first saw rain hail, I thought it was the end of the world. After all, everything was so new.

I started school two weeks later. I was excited, but I also felt scared because I didn't know what would happen to me. My first day went very well even though I couldn't understand anything anyone was saying, my first language at the time being English. In class, I tried to follow the lessons despite how difficult it was. During class, I would simply observe what others were doing. If I saw that everyone was standing, I would stand, if everyone was laughing, I would laugh. It was very funny, but by doing that I felt comfortable and equal to them.

When you are seven years old, the only thing you want in life is to be carefree, but unfortunately in my case, I couldn't be like that and the main reason was that I needed to work a double job. My parents couldn't speak the language so I couldn't rely on them, so I had to use a bit of cunning.

Every time I would visit my cousins, I would make an effort to speak Italian with them even though they wanted to learn, more than anything else, what little I could say in Twii, one of the Ghanaian dialects.

Not only did I use my cousins, but I was lucky enough to have an old lady, Emilia, live near my house. Every evening around six o'clock, she would pass by my house to go for a walk. One day, I greeted her and that very evening she invited me to walk with her. My parents allowed it and from then on, every evening at 6 pm, Emilia would call me and we would go for a walk; she wanted company and I wanted to learn the language.

In the following years, everything seemed to be going well until I reached the age of 14–15 when I had to choose what college I wanted to go to. Nobody could give me much help with this. During that time,

I hoped to have an older sibling who could guide me, but I had to do it alone. I enrolled in one of the most difficult schools in the country, but I didn't do it because everybody would say 'wow', but because it was the school that could help me get to where I wanted to be.

College is where my insecurities came out both physically and mentally. During PE class, the teacher would demand some sort of acrobatics exercise that seemed impossible to me, and as I watched my classmates succeed, I felt like a failure. When I tried, everybody used to laugh at me, and my only reaction was to smile, but they didn't know how much it really hurt me; PE became my enemy. I thought that to be able to do all the activities properly I had to lose weight. Not only did school make me feel 'fat', but my mother's friends also made me feel that way. I started lying to my parents about eating at school so I wouldn't eat dinner. This continued until I got seriously ill and I still never told my parents why I stopped eating because I was ashamed, but I knew that my mom knew why.

Teachers also used to never like my oral and writing tests. People say you shouldn't compare yourself to others, but sometimes you do. This issue made me feel more insecure every single day and I would panic anytime I had an oral test because the teacher would stare at me like I had done something wrong.

At the age of 17, I changed classes because I wanted to learn more aside from economics and languages (French) and IT (the worst course I could ever choose for myself). In the classroom, I felt invisible, not understood and alone.

Then my mom became ill at work and although we have been in the country for a long time, she still couldn't speak Italian fluently like I could, so I had to take her to the GP and translate. From what appeared to just be an issue with her knees, turned out up to be something else entirely. I ended up having to skip school quite often to take her to the hospital. At school, I explained what was happening at home, and I tried everything I could to recap the lessons I missed, but it wasn't easy. When I asked my friends to tell me, nobody would answer me or they would just give me the wrong information – I never knew why. This frustrated me a lot because I didn't know what to do. As a result of this, my grades started to drop, so I had to do extra lessons after school and I would stay up till the morning to study and do extra homework for Math and English.

One day that I will never forget, and that changed me completely. My math teacher had given us our math exams results and I didn't get the grade I was expecting. I felt ashamed and felt like a failure. Not only did I receive a bad grade, but also two of my friends that were sitting next to me. My teacher told them that they wouldn't have to worry and after the Christmas holidays, she would explain to them what went wrong. After that, I was expecting something from her but she ignored me and went back to her desk. I was devastated, I wasn't expecting it at all. I asked her if we could have a chat outside, and told her what happened and if she could help me to understand what I did wrong, she said, "Sorry, I can't help you." You can imagine how I felt. My Christmas was not great, because I was full of sad emotions and I was giving up on everything.

However, in March 2019, I came with my dad to the UK, just for three days of holiday; I fell in love with it. When I came back home, the issues remained the same and one day after school I got tired of everything and, in tears, I went home and told my mom everything, but it was probably too late. I wasn't surprised when they failed me in that class. I told my parents that I didn't want to go back to that school and that I wanted to move to the UK. Before moving, I decided to start working, a decision against my dad's wishes, to help him out at home. Having now spent 11 years in Italy with him being the only one working to look after us. I worked for a month and a half in customer service. I didn't decide to work just to help my dad, but I also wanted to put myself out there. I had a fear of speaking in front of people

Why did I choose the UK? I wanted to be in another country where I could feel valued as a person and proud of my colour. The day I was moving to the UK, I knew that I was about to leave 11 years of my life behind that was full of happiness, sadness, friendship, family and neighbours. On the plane, I cried. I didn't know what to expect here in the UK. When I moved, I had one issue – language. My first language was, and still is, Italian, so I had to start from scratch all over again.

As soon as I arrived, my uncle took me to Oldham College, and on the way there he talked to me about apprenticeships and I became interested. Unfortunately, when I went to ask about this type of opportunity I was told that since I had only been in the UK for a short time I couldn't do it due to having to be there for at least three years. However, they agreed to enlist me full time. At first, I was sceptical, because I didn't want to do long school hours like I did in Italy, but they told me that I would only have to attend school three times a week for a few hours and I accepted. To tell the truth, I didn't know what would happen to me when I started on this new path, but I was ready to fight for it.

The week after school began, the school called me and talked about an apprenticeship programme, and as my English was not great, I said yes anyway. That day I came to school to learn more about it was the beginning of my new life path, but of course, I didn't know that. To be honest, I only understood that the programme was called Leadership Through Sport and Business and that they helped 16–21-year-olds enter the world of work. I took part in a debate on Brexit and also did an interview.

I don't know what came over me that day, but I faced it with courage. I wanted to throw away all the insecurity.

Becky Willson

I hope that my story resonates with anyone with health conditions, mental illness, or learning disabilities. I want you to know that you are more than your conditions, illnesses or disabilities. They may limit what you can do, but they do not define your dreams or who you are. You are strong for living life the way you are. Be yourself and keep heading towards your goals. Now, more than ever, anything is achievable.

I Do Have Worth

I grew up being bullied for who I was; a child with hearing loss, health conditions that meant missing too much school and undiagnosed autism that made me feel like an outcast around my peers 24/7. Instead of being able to express myself verbally, I expressed myself through art, performing on stage, reading and writing. I let these creative passions and friends I had met on the way help me to start accepting who I was.

I was unique and not someone who had to change to fit in. I could wear my hearing aids with pride because who cared if I got mocked, I could finally hear. I would finish writing books after books; I would create art pieces that later got hung up in an exhibition; I would belt out the highest notes and act my best on stage because none of these were flaws, they were unique skills I had acquired from being me.

That is when I ran into a new challenge. My Educators.

I joined a college to start professionally learning how to be a stage performer, as it had been one of my dreams since being a child. I was accepted onto this course, but as a 'Wild Card'. That should have been a red flag, but with my new-found confidence in myself I powered on into learning.

My peers were nothing like me, but this was something I was used to; however, I should not have been worried about my peers this time, but the Head Educator of this course.

My health declined, and every day got a little bit harder to get through but with pure drive and love, I went into my college not batting an eyelid to these new investigations and new doctors that I had in my life. Until I got very sick for the Christmas Showcase.

I was meant to play one of the leads, but the day of the show I got exceptionally ill and was not allowed to perform and had to rest following a relapse of glandular fever. I thought this would not change anything for me, but it did. From then, I was treated differently at this college by that one Head Educator, who should have been my support but was far from it.

We were casting for our next show, *Chicago*, and I was auditioning for Roxie. I made it into the top three students to be decided for this role but was quickly cast aside due to being too much of a risk to cast, thanks to my health. This behaviour I was used to by peers my own age, not adults who were meant to lead us into being our best selves and performers.

Through dedication, I still worked backstage with my friends in the production team. I was not told to be at the shows, or expected, and when I did arrive early every day to help with the show, the Head of Course barely batted an eyelid my way as if I was not even his student. Everyone in the class got a rose after that week but me. Everyone got a congratulations and thank you but me. It was as if I wasn't even there.

Yet, my dream of being on stage professionally was far greater than one person who told me I could not. When I got my new diagnoses and my health symptoms finally had some names, this changed. These diagnoses made the Head of the Performing Arts course tell me not come back next year, and if I did, he would simply turn me away and not teach me. No one would hire a performer with medical conditions such as mine, and I should forget about ever being on stage.

Just like that, my dream to be a performer was crushed. I was tough though and turned my attention to the other things I loved like my writing, art and reading. I started writing new books, drew in sketchbooks that I had collected and read book after book, only these hobbies were starting to get harder to do with that one recurring thought going around and around in my head.

"No one will hire you with health conditions like yours." I started losing hope in the things I love, and that I would never be able to make a career out of them; I would never be able to make a career out of anything. Even when I went to university after all odds this thought stayed.

My chosen course was in Journalism, Advertising and Marketing, chosen through my love for creative writing, as well as writing random essays on my strange and unique fascinations that I had such as dreams, the 80s and American pop culture. Even with ups and downs with my health and a few visits to A&E during that year, I was able to finish the year with a high 2:1. I was close to feeling that hope again.

That is when my Head of Course met with me; the most lovely and supportive lady I had met in my educational years. She recognised my creativity and the way I wrote my essays, and recommended I change my degree to English, something I had never thought of doing.

To this day, I wish I had not taken this advice.

I had English professors that were stuck in their old ways of teaching that they would not make arrangements for students with learning difficulties, health conditions and hearing loss such as myself.

One professor was amazing, printing off the presentation slides of every lecture, and helping me with notes if I ever missed anything with my hearing or if I had to be at an appointment at the doctors. I treasured this professor, as she was the only one in the entire course to do this. Unfortunately, one professor had a different attitude. She told me that unless I had a diagnosis down on paper to prove I needed extra support that she would not make changes to her teaching methods.

I was back to feeling hopeless. Through the struggle, the meetings and the low grades, no matter how hard I tried on each essay and how many times I read the articles and chapters we were studying, I got advised to drop out. Being advised to drop out, is just a kinder way to kick someone out of university in my opinion. The university said I could come back next year, but that did not mean anything would change.

Within that next year, I got a diagnosis of High Functioning Autism, but it was too late. My hope for going back to university or any education was gone. However, part of me never stopped fighting to prove them all wrong. I wanted to prove to that Head of Performing Arts teacher that I could make it, even though I had health conditions. I wanted to prove to that English professor that I was smart, and I did not need to work to textbook perfection in order to be successful.

I enrolled in the Prince's Trust who saw me for who I was and helped me explore where I was talented and where I needed some help. There, I found the hope that I had been lacking, even when a new diagnosis came my way that crushed my hope again, they found a way to bring me back up and restore my hope.

I started drawing again, buying myself an iPad to create digital pieces of art. I started writing again, book ideas flowing. I started performing again, not in shows or on stage, but in my room or around the house, singing to the musicals I had once trained to be in.

Then, Prince's Trust found me a traineeship at a large technology company. I had to pass a couple of interviews and team activities to prove I was worth hiring, but for the first time in a long time, I was not worried. When I pulled up at that train station to catch the bus to the interview, I wasn't afraid to be myself.

Being myself was exactly what they were looking for. I was hired, made Team Leader, was put into a department for the company and created promotional content for events that were happening all over the site. I used my art and the lessons I had learned through my one year doing marketing and advertising. My so-called weirdness and qualities that I thought would get me nowhere, were loved and an asset to the department.

I had a purpose and dream again. I had real hope for myself.

Months after the traineeship I was hired as an intern for the company, in the same department I had worked in before. I felt solid for the first time in a long time.

My new colleagues and manager understood my medical conditions, my autism and hearing loss. They made sure to put things in place so that I could be the best employee I could be, without letting any of my conditions let myself or the company down.

I know now where I belong and my worth. I know that I can be an asset to a team. I can use my skills for professional use, and not just as a hobby. I know that I am not a 'Wild Card' but someone that is not a risk at all.

Even after the internship and I'm living unemployed in a pandemic, I still have that worth and I hope I never lose it again.

TG Consulting Ltd is an independent consultancy that specialises in connecting educators, students and employers. Our ethos is to connect, collaborate and create.

Our services include:

Graduate and student employability training and coaching
Embedding employability frameworks and modelling
Graduate outcomes strategy
Employability and Careers service health checks
Employer engagement alignment
Programme analysis
TEF Performance improvement and submissions
Institutional portfolio reviews

We understand the higher education and student environment well and can provide useful insights into the higher education space including the student journey and recent trends. This will align your campaigns and products so you can have a clear proposition, targeted solution and engaging campaign.

Some of our services in this space include:

- Recruitment campaign consultation
- Talent attraction strategies
- Higher education insights
- Student voice campaigns

We offer a range of services from short-term or strategic support to aligning services and team structures, so whatever your project, drop us a line and we will connect, collaborate and create.

info@tgconsultingltd.co.uk
www.tgconsultingltd.co.uk
Find us on Twitter, Instagram and LinkedIn

Helpful Organisations

This book is full of inspirational stories to celebrate the strength of these brave individuals who have overcome adversity in their lifetime. The content of this book is not intended to be a substitute for professional advice or treatment. Always seek the advice of a mental health professional or other qualified health practitioner.

Useful resources

Student Space
https://www.studentspace.org.uk/

Student Minds
https://www.studentminds.org.uk/

Youth UK
https://www.ukyouth.org/

Children's Society
https://www.childrenssociety.org.uk/

NHS – Call 111 (UK only)
https://www.nhs.uk/conditions/stress-anxiety-depression/student-mental-health/

Teen Mental Health Org
https://www.teenmentalhealth.org

The Samaritans
https://www.samaritans.org.uk

Prevention of Young Suicide
https://www.papyrus-uk.org

Mind for Better Mental Health
https://www.mind.org.uk